SOCIAL SECURITY

SOCIAL
SECURITY

The Fraud in Your Future

WARREN SHORE

MACMILLAN PUBLISHING CO., INC.
NEW YORK

COLLIER MACMILLAN PUBLISHERS
LONDON

Macmillan Publishing Co., Inc.
866 Third Avenue, New York, N.Y. 10022
Collier Macmillan Canada, Ltd.

Library of Congress Cataloging in Publication Data

Shore, Warren.
     Social security: the fraud in your future.

     Includes index.
     1. United States.   Social Security Administration.
2. Social Security—United States.   I. Title.
HD7125.S53   368.4′00973   75-16444
ISBN 0-02-610550-0

FIRST PRINTING 1975

Printed in the United States of America

For Jack

Contents

BOOK II
A Way Out

Acknowledgments

This book is the product of many people who were angry enough, creative enough, expert enough, and kind enough to help. Bernard Zion was always there, either to listen to a new idea, criticize an old one, or just to stand by, ready to make an endless succession of new charts. Professor Milton Friedman made his wealth of knowledge available on the gamble that I would see this through. The same is true of Professors Colin Campbell, Roman Weil, and Robert Kaplan. Chuck Hobbs has not only done some of the most original thinking on the subject of Social Security, but even better, he shares and communicates. John Brittain, of the Brookings Institute, put his vast knowledge of economic theory and history at my disposal. No one writing on the subject of women's finances should be without the advice of Dee Dee Ahern, or for that matter, her warm concern. No matter what the barbs contained in these pages for Social Security Administration policy, my requests for information were always handled professionally and accurately by Mike Naver, Jim Brown, Dave Kading, Jake Krch, and John Yakimo. To the others within the administration who felt that publicly helping would cost their jobs, my profound thanks for your risk—and superb information. The early research of Alvern Engwall was more valuable than he would admit. My conversations with psychologist Edward Ruda added humanity to a subject always threatening to dry out. I was crazy about Liz Pryde even before she made herself available as tax-expert-always-on-call. To the library staff of the U.S. Commerce and U.S. Labor departments, my congratulations and thanks. Moving ideas from conversation to print requires solid professionals willing to help. I am grateful for Richard Hainey and Arthur Pine, who are and did. Finally, to Thursday, my long-nurtured thanks for his boundless confidence and support in whatever measure it was needed. And to my wife, who remained charming while learning to fall asleep to a lullaby of typing, my wish for joy.

BOOK I

The Promise

PART I

The Federal Version

1] *Behind the Trust Funds*

Just inside the sky-blue booklet printed by the federal Social Security Administration, there is a single sentence:

> Nine out of ten working people in the United States are now building protection for themselves and their families under the Social Security program.

The great majority of Americans believe that sentence to be true. Whether or not we have actually read the government booklet called *Your Social Security,* which contains the sentence, most of us have decided to believe. We tell the government we believe every time we accept a paycheck with a Social Security deduction in the little box marked "FICA" (for Federal Insurance Contribution Act).

Believing that sentence is the most expensive single decision most of us will make during our lives. The average American is betting more than $100,000 of his earnings that the sky-blue booklet is right, and he is counting on his children to bet twice that much.

But the sentence is *not* true, With every passing pay period, those nine-out-of-ten working people are *losing* protection for themselves and their families. The fact is the American Social Security system is neither insurance nor a contribution, and the price of believing that it is grows every day.

The system that was once a symbol for financial stability has, during the last five years, become a major factor in the American recession. While government spokesmen blame the nation's slow-down on a 51 percent rise in the cost of gasoline and an 80 percent rise in the cost of heating oil since 1970, no mention is made that Social Security taxes have risen an incredible 121 percent during the same time. The program the Social Security Administration so proudly labels "tax-free" is in fact full of double taxation, hidden taxation, and destructive limitations. Social Security has been quietly changed into a monster.

It will not be easy for most Americans to accept the fact that Social Security no longer works. For nearly forty years the pro-gram has grown steadily in the public consciousness to a point where it seems to represent government itself—a vast and unknow-able collection of laws and men that seem to promise "everything will be all right" if we simply demonstrate good faith by paying and voting.

Thus, for most of us, to doubt Social Security is to ask of government the unthinkable: Why should we believe what you're telling us? What really makes it true? How much better could we do on our own? What is the real cost to the nation?

That's what this book is about. It is to show that blind faith can't make you secure no matter whom or what you have faith in; that your questions about Social Security have logical and direct answers; and that some of these answers are so frightening the government would rather you didn't ask them. You can do much better on your own.

But the book is also about joy. The joy that you can know about what is important to you, and that knowing will bring control and finally change. We'll talk about workable changes later.

To begin, then, we have to establish the difference between what the federal government wants us to believe about Social Security and what the evidence shows to be true.

Social Security is a promise. When the federal government takes money from your paycheck for the program, it does so with the promise that it will use the money in your best interest; that is, the money will insure that you will have a retirement income, a death benefit, and disability protection—everything the law seems to guarantee.

Your future, then, depends on the quality of that promise. You will, after all, stop working some day, but you will continue to have expenses. You will die some day and perhaps leave heirs who will continue to have expenses. The federal promise, then, had better come true.

The promise of the Social Security Administration to the American working public is based on the following paragraph from *Your Social Security*:

> The basic idea of social security is a simple one: During the working years employees, their employers, and self-employed people pay social security contributions which are pooled in special trust funds. When earnings stop or are reduced because the worker retires, becomes disabled, or dies, monthly cash benefits are paid to replace part of the earnings the family has lost.

It all comes down to that paragraph. Though total Social Security legislation fills more than forty volumes of complex case law and constantly updated rulings, the "life" of the program springs from that little paragraph.

The ability of the federal government to do what it claims to be doing is exactly the same as its ability to follow that paragraph —no more and no less. Yet so much of that short, seemingly simple, paragraph is either wholly wrong, partially wrong, or intentionally misleading that most of this book will be devoted to telling what it really means.

Take the words "trust fund," for instance. By generally accepted legal definition a trust is "a legal title to property held by one party [the trustee] for the benefit of another [the beneficiary]." The definition is so simple, in fact, that most Americans (questioned in a 1973 *New York Times* national survey) believe that they "own" the money that the Social Security Administration takes from their paychecks. That is, after all, what a trust fund is supposed to be. And since the government continues calling the payroll deductions "contributions" instead of taxes, what else can we believe?

The truth is there is no trust fund and hasn't been for years. To be sure there is a quantity of money in an account labeled "Old Age and Survivors, Disability Insurance Trust Fund," but that label alone is not enough to insure that the money in the account is truly in trust for you. To distinguish between the label and the reality of the Social Security trust fund, we simply need to look at how trust funds are normally handled and compare this with the federal government's handling of your trust fund.

A trust fund is an amount of money with a specific job to do. Making the fund grow, or at least remain stable enough to do the job intended, requires a good deal of prudent professional care and some financial luck. There are, however, four statements we should be able to make about all trust funds:

1. *The fund should grow at least at the rate that the population it protects is growing.* This means that if ten people have contributed to a trust fund which makes an essentially equal promise to all of them, before the fund's managers can extend the promise to twenty contributors the fund itself must at least have doubled.

2. *The fund should grow at least at the rate its promise grows.* This means you shouldn't believe a fund manager who tells you that a certain pile of money will suddenly

guarantee a bigger and more expensive promise—without adding any more money.

3. *The fund should be adequate to do its job with only a small fraction of its assets used in any given year.* Thus, you can consider your fund too small for its job if it uses up most of its assets in a single year.

4. *The fund should be owned by those who contributed to it or by those they designate.* This means that the trustee should not be allowed ownership of the fund, since his goals are not the same as the owners'. Where ownership is not clear, the contributors to a fund can expect that the fund will stop doing what they anticipated and may even subvert their goals.

These four rules are basic. Honest financial managers agree that while adherence to the four does not guarantee a fund's success, ignoring even one of the rules for very long is a sure invitation to disaster. By this criterion the Social Security Administration's so-called trust fund is a unique financial flop. By every aspect of all four rules the fund is a longtime failure—if it was ever a trust fund at all.

Again, don't mistake the four guidelines for brittle niceties of finance. They are simply the least one should expect from a sum of money before conferring upon it the title "trust fund." Without them no fund can exist.

Now consider the sum of money which the federal government says is guaranteeing your future:

In 1960 the total assets of the Social Security trust funds stood at $22.6 billion which were to insure the benefits of some 67.5 million American workers.

By 1966 the working population "covered" by Social Security trust funds had swelled, by legislative and employment increases, to 76 million—a rise of 12.6 percent.

In order to have kept pace with the covered population increase (as required under rule 1), the Social Security trust funds should have grown by $2.8 billion to $25.4 billion. Instead, the total assets in the funds dropped by more than $300 million during the six-year period to $22.3 billion.

One of the major skills necessary in learning to hear what the government is saying to us is overcoming our awe of "big numbers." Citizens used to dealing with money on the level of family economics become strangely numb when the discussion turns to billions and trillions as though these vast quantities would somehow not respond to normal arithmetic. How else could the events between 1960 and 1966 have failed to cause an anguished outcry? The federal planners were saying "two and two is eight" and no one stood up to correct them.

Even though the example involved is years old, it's worth looking at as classic bureaucratic double-think. Once we learn the language it will pass out of use—not before.

In 1960, an election year, the Congress and the Social Security Administration declared that assets of $22.6 billion were the "guarantee" that Social Security's trusts would pay the nation's 67.5 million covered work force all the government had promised. Yet six years later, while the work force increased by 12.6 percent, the trust funds stood 1.4 percent lower than before. During each of the years the Social Security Administration declared in its annual report that its so-called trust fund was "adequate" and "solvent."

But how could that be? If $22.6 billion represented solvency in 1960, then a fund of $22.3 billion covering more workers (promised higher benefits) must be less "solvent"—less "adequate." By rule 1 alone, the funds had become 14 percent less able to do the job promised in 1960. But each year it had been given a clean bill of financial health. And each year we listened but didn't hear.

Nor does the story end there. Remember, there are two ways in which a financial promise can be weakened: either make the same promise to more people or make a bigger promise—all with the same money.

In 1960 the total Social Security benefit payments for the year were $11.2 billion. This, remember, was at a time when the Social

Security trust funds stood at $22.6 billion—or roughly enough to have paid benefits for slightly more than two years. But 1960 was also an important election year, when promises are more likely to fill the air than discussions of tax increases. As it turned out, 1962, 1964, and 1966 were also rich with tight congressional races and the accompanying need to please the home districts.

By 1965 Social Security benefits had expanded to $18.3 billion—an astounding 63 percent increase in five years. Without official explanation, the trust funds fell behind. The 1965 level had sunk to $19.8 billion or an average loss, since 1960, of $266 million every year.

As 1966 began, the Social Security trust funds stood at a level where they could underwrite benefit payments for only thirteen months—a decline of more than 46 percent in time-value of the funds during a single five-year period.

In all five years the numbers were posted and distributed from the Baltimore, Maryland, headquarters of Social Security. In all five years the funds were pronounced "sound" and "stable."

In 1966, with Social Security benefit payments 79 percent higher than only six years previous and the total cash in the funds 1 percent lower (an 80 percent impairment in less than seventy months' time), the commissioner of the Social Security Administration declared the funds "the heart of the American social security system," labeling their future "assured."

What gives bureaucrats the confidence to pronounce "down" as if it meant "up"? Perhaps it is the confidence that we aren't listening or don't care. What else could explain the events between the years 1957 and 1965 when the yearly benefits bill for Social Security tripled (from $6 billion to $18 billion); the working population, promised those payments, increased by 20 percent; and the cash in the trust funds actually *dropped* in six out of those nine years!

But the quality of the federal promise to American workers, as embodied in those funds, is at its lowest ebb today and can only become worse.

The Social Security trust funds that in 1947 could guarantee payments for more than seventeen years can now assure only nine months' benefits checks. In spite of tax increases of more than 100 percent in the last four years, the net increase in the Social Security trust funds has become less in every one of those years.

By any stretch of economic logic, at least two of our original four rules for trust funds have been systematically shattered by the federal government. Too much has been promised to too many. The last two rules are not only the simplest to understand, but offer the clearest lesson for those who wish to know how the federal establishment wants us to think.

The yearly obligations of a stable trust fund should remain a small fraction of the fund's size. Applying this rule simply, a $1,000 trust fund should not have annual expenses or obligations exceeding, say, $100.

The federal government is so sure of this principle that both the Federal Trade Commission and the Interstate Commerce Commission regularly issue bulletins to state insurance officials warning that they be on guard against insurance companies which violate the rule.

Says the latest Federal Trade Commission trust and reserve account evaluation bulletin: ". . . the right to make promises to the public must be maintained as financially sacred through a reserve system able to withstand pressure." What the FTC means is that groups such as insurance companies sell promises and that the federal government is on hand to see that adequate reserves exist so that the promises are kept.

Since the Social Security Administration admits to having made promises to the American public of nearly $3 trillion (even if no new workers come into the system), it's tempting to compare them with private insurance in terms of reserves/benefit ratio. Indeed the administration invited the comparison in 1974 when, in a strongly worded defense of its own methods, the newspaper public was told to "think of social security as group insurance."

Very well then, take a look: At the end of 1973, the total life insurance in force in the United States was $1.8 trillion. This amount was backed by total reserves of $208 billion—slightly more than 10 percent. The same essential relationship existed in 1974.

For the minimum $2.9 trillion (some estimates put the total at $4 trillion) in "insurance" that Social Security had in force during 1974, the "reserves" come to $44.5 billion—less than 1 percent.

Can a trust fund truly be worthy of the name when it represents less than 1 percent of the promises in force? New York State Superintendent of Insurance, Benjamin R. Schenck, said in early 1974:

> Where a reserve account is less than 10 percent of insurance in force, someone is betting too heavily on the future with somebody else's money. We would begin an immediate investigation, with an eye toward suspending company operations, if that were tried in New York.

Listen carefully. The federal bureaucracy is talking to us again. They are saying, "Think of Social Security as insurance because you are paying for a future promise, just as with insurance. But don't judge Social Security as you would insurance because—well, just don't."

The trust-fund myth won't hold up no matter which comparison is used to judge. The next most pertinent measure is the relationship between benefits paid out in a year and the reserves on hand during that same year. In a recent survey conducted by the American Risk and Insurance Association, state insurance commissioners agreed that a company paying yearly benefits equal to "more than 15% of its reserve account" had a "major impairment" of that account to look forward to.

Keep that survey in mind as we look at the last six years of the system federal officials want us "to think of as group insurance."

In 1969 United States private insurance companies paid a total of $15.5 billion in benefit payments to policyholders. This included death benefits, disability payments, and annuity/retirement payments. The sum represents 9.8 percent of the $158 billion in private reserves that year.

During that same year Social Security distributed $26.7 billion, an amount equal to 78 percent of the $34.1 billion in reserve. The following chart continues the grim story.

	BENEFITS AS A PERCENTAGE OF RESERVES	
Year	*Private Insurance*	*Social Security*
1970	9.8%	84%
1971	9.8%	92%
1972	9.7%	97%

Thus by 1972 the U.S. Social Security system was distributing money at a rate six times higher than the rate that would have closed a private insurance company. Still Washington administrators called it insurance and labeled the insurance "sound."

As an ever-watchful federal and state bureaucracy continues to monitor, private insurance has maintained a 9 percent to 10 percent benefits-to-reserves ratio through 1973 and 1974.

In 1973 and 1974 the remains of the Social Security trust-fund myth should have exploded, but once again did not. While paying more than $53 billion in benefits during 1973, the Social Security system achieved the unique status of giving out *more* than the trust funds contained—an absurd benefits-to-reserve percentage of 114 percent. In 1974 benefit checks equaled a withering 133 percent of the reserves once dubbed "the heart of the Social Security system." If so, the heart was being cut out to feed the patient and this seemed to make him sicker.

We're in danger here of being bogged down in numbers and missing the point. The value of all these calculations is not to make Americans trust-fund experts, but good listeners—people who can make a government promise stand still and be counted.

The "promise" of the Social Security trust funds can't be

counted on because the so-called pool we're told they represent doesn't exist. That single fact is not as much financial as it is political. If the funds aren't guaranteeing the system, what is?

The real clue to the trust-fund mystery lies in the almost off-hand remarks from the 1972 report of the board of trustees for the Social Security system to the U.S. Congress.

If we listen carefully to the trustees' remarks, all the apparent inconsistencies we've observed about the trust funds will become clear. Without intending to, they reveal who really pays the bill.

In commenting on the condition of the trust funds (which then stood at $42.7 billion), the report said:

> Because compulsory social insurance is assured of continuing income (new workers must come into the program), it does not have to build up the kind of reserves that are necessary at all times in an institution that cannot count on current income to meet current obligations.

The report went on to conclude that "the kind of reserves" which are correct for Social Security are "about one year in benefits."

These remarks may seem like just another dreary conclusion in an endless stream of murky government proceedings, but they contain the clear and brutal truth about your future. The trust funds are a phony. When it became obvious that the money once labeled the life of the system was dwindling rapidly into insignificance, a new "life" had to be found. Thus, it is calmly proclaimed from Washington that it was never trust funds that guarantee future benefits, but compulsion. "New workers must come into the system," we're told, so we need only a token reserve.

Though few took note at the time, the Taxpayers' Federation (a long-respected lobby group) looked horror-stricken at the 1972 trustees' report in a press release issued that year:

> It is now publicly acknowledged [lamented the Federation], that all adherence to sound insurance practices has been abandoned.

This single decision assures ever-mounting tax bills for the system without any possibility of relief.

The lid was finally off. In a single public adjustment of bureaucratic thought (obviously practiced for many years before this), the trust-fund mystery evaporated. There was no need for the trust fund to grow as the working (covered) population grew, because it was not the funds, but the workers, that guaranteed the system. The federal government could "compel" them to do so. The funds could remain stagnant as benefits exploded, not because this is the way trust funds act, but because the government (unlike private insurance companies) could "be assured" of selling new policies every year. They have, after all, the ultimate fiscal tool—compulsion.

The insane benefits-to-reserves ratios of the seventies (paying out more than the total in the funds) needn't concern us, we're told, "because the concept of acturial soundness in a compulsory insurance system differs" from what we had been reassured earlier to believe.

In short, the so-called trust funds didn't act like trust funds because they never were in trust for us. The largest earmarked cache in the history of the U.S. federal treasury turned out to be nothing but a vast political slush fund enabling Congress after Congress to buy votes by promising to give away more than existed. Nor was the Congress alone. It has taken years of willingness by various government agencies to manipulate the facts of Social Security into a program that sounded possible.

Before we continue discussing the effect of government lies on the rest of your life, we should take a look at how the illusions are accomplished. The methods of inducing a collective trance on a nation about an issue so vital to its future are both subtle and venally obvious. Take care that you don't begin admiring the tactics used against you—they are that crafty.

2] The Manipulators

It is one of those regrettable facts of modern life that your government is no longer the same as "you." Though it was inevitable, as the nation grew, that the intimate town council would gradually withdraw and expand into legislatures, bureaus, congressional committees, and presidential councils, government has become more than simply big. The federal government has become "they" and we must learn to keep that in mind.

The federal bureaucracy deals more with itself than it does with the public. As such its concerns become internal. To its participants the normal urge to perpetuate and expand their way of life means to perpetuate and expand government. That is not the same as what you want.

To continue to leave the federal government to its own devices on the faith that "they can only stay in power with our votes, so they must be on our side" is an expensive rationalization. It ignores the many similarities between big government and those sectors of private industry we've learned to be wary of.

Our government buys more supplies and services, sells more bonds, owns more assets, employs more people, and takes in more money than any of the corporations we entrust it to regulate. Can we assume that a bureaucracy will always act on our behalf simply because it must curry our favor? It would be the same as assuming that General Motors officers will always make decisions in the public interest simply because they depend on public approval.

The fact is that both the big corporation and big government learn to deal with information so as to promote their own self-interest and minimize interference. But whose "covered up" mistakes are more dangerous to you?—the organization that must pay for its errors with its own assets, or the organization with the power to take your assets?

The power of the government to manipulate its own output of information is so complete that a problem can be done away with by simply declaring it not a problem and never discussing it again.

Thus in 1972, when the Social Security trustees announced that a trust fund roughly equal to "one year's benefits" was adequate to meet our needs, they put to rest in their minds the nagging fact of a dwindling sum of money.

The principle involved is called "Anything We Do Is Right" and is used often when seeming contradictions get in the way of what some consider progress. It is set in motion this way:

In 1972 the total Social Security trust funds were enough to pay benefits for 12.3 months and so it was in that year that "one year's benefits" was declared the right amount for them to be.

In 1947, when the funds would have paid benefits for seventeen years, the Social Security Administration declared the fund's balance itself as proof the plan was sound. But every year the fund's ability to guarantee future payments, with its balance, fell.

The perfect year to tell American taxpayers that government compulsion—and not money—is what makes Social Security work was 1972. During the previous twenty years the trust fund balance had fallen from being worth five years' benefits to being worth around one year's benefits—and now was headed still lower.

"One year's benefits" has a nice fiscal ring to it, as though the trustees or the administration intended to maintain that level in some kind of annualized budgeting. But it wasn't to last. In 1973 the funds equaled only 10.3 months' benefits, but no mention was made in the trustees' report of falling below "our one year minimum" or any such language. In fact the time/use of the funds wasn't mentioned at all.

Nor was it mentioned in the 1974 report that the funds had slipped to a level where they would cover slightly more than nine months' payments or that for 1975 the amount on hand would underwrite only eight months' checks and that the 1976 administration forecast was for no more than seven months' payments "in trust for our future."

Actually the only year in which "one year's benefits" was officially declared "adequate" to fund our $3 trillion Social Security system was in 1972 when the funds happened to equal one year's benefits. By official forecast of the 1974 General Accounting Office audit of the Social Security Administration, the trust funds will never again equal as much as one year's benefits.

It's obvious that 1972 was the perfect year to tell us we needn't bother to watch the fund balance ("Anything We Do Is Right"), but did the trustees know something else about the trust funds that they weren't telling us?

In the 1974 trustees' report to the House of Representatives Ways and Means Committee (dated June 3, 1974), House members were told that the trust fund would no longer grow at all—in either real or percentage-of-benefits terms, and that in fact by 1977 the funds would show their first drop in over twelve years. The funds would then continue to dissipate, Congress was told, in spite of crushing Social Security tax increases of more than 255 percent projected between 1970 and 1978—more than all other federal tax increases combined.

The report so alarmed Senator Carl T. Curtis (R-Nebraska),

senior member of the Senate Finance Committee, that on June 13, 1974 he asked the Social Security Administration to tell him just how much the total trust-fund deficit was expected to be.

The answer came on July 26, 1974 directly to Senator Curtis's Senate office (without accompanying press release). The cumulative deficit in Social Security funding would "exceed $60 billion" by 1979.

No more need be said about why we stopped hearing about trust-fund "time/benefit levels" after 1972. The American public needed to be weaned quickly from the notion that trust funds guarantee benefits, because trust funds were on their way out.

There is currently (1975) less than $50 billion in United States bonds on hand in the Social Security trust funds. By the Social Security Administration's own analysis, the trust funds will be gone by 1980.

It is appropriate to mention here that in an interoffice directive from the Social Security Administration's Office of Information to the U.S. Government Printing Office (in mid-1973) "no changes are contemplated in the major text" of the booklet *Your Social Security.*

We are still to be told our wages and earnings "are pooled in special trust funds" for our future even though the funds' future, as of this writing, is less than forty-eight months.

Still, the booklet can always be changed later when reality catches up to all the promises. It has happened before.

As late as 1965 Social Security Administration publications contained the following sentence "explaining" how the program works: ". . . when earnings stop or are reduced because the worker retires, dies or becomes disabled, monthly cash benefits are paid from the funds to replace part of the earnings the family has lost."

Since the worst dwindling of the funds was occurring during those years (in six out of nine years between 1957 and 1965 the funds lost ground to rising costs), the fiction could not be maintained that "funds" were actually paying benefits.

The problem was handled in typical bureaucratic fashion. If

a situation won't seem to go away, change the way it's described. Thus the phrase "from the funds" was dropped from all Social Security Administration documents and has never appeared since.

The Social Security Administration likes to think of itself as running an insurance plan, but more importantly it wants you to think of Social Security as insurance. To this end the administration's vast public relations staff never misses a chance to drive home the idea that Social Security and "insurance" are the same thing.

In the administration pamphlet describing the Social Security card, we are told, "Your card is the symbol of your insurance policy under the federal Social Security Law."

At least thirty-five times in the sixty-one current Social Security Administration booklets describing the system, taxes, removed from payroll checks before a worker ever sees them, are referred to as either "contributions" or "premiums."

In a 1973 paper defending the system, Wilbur J. Cohen, former secretary of Health, Education, and Welfare and generally conceded to be the architect of American Social Security, repeatedly called the current plan "government insurance," adding that it is a "legal right to benefits backed by a guarantee from the federal government and legal recourse to the courts for payment"—just like insurance.

In fifty-three separate references contained in Social Security pamphlets published during 1974, we hear that our payroll tax money is being "pooled" and that "contributions paid to the pool" are available later to replace lost earnings.

To sum up, we are constantly asked to accept Social Security as an "insurance plan" whose "contributions" or "premiums" are "pooled" for us within a system "guaranteed" by the government with "legal recourse in the courts" to imply that we own a right to the benefits promised.

If the foregoing statement were true, Social Security would indeed be insurance. But the statement is simply an example of many manipulators working together to produce a thought almost entirely false

As soon as the government's insurance myth for Social Security is examined it begins to disintegrate. But as we've seen before, there is a strong bureaucratic notion that words create their own reality—that if Social Security can be made to sound like real insurance, it will somehow protect us better. Let's take the obvious misstatements first.

If any grade school student were asked to define the word "contributions" as applied to money, he would find himself including in his thoughts the concept of "voluntary." We don't make "contributions" to a burglar or to the local traffic court after a parking ticket. Where threat or force is implied, we are correct to be insulted at the use of the word "contribution."

Yet in spite of a very clear federal law making it a felony for either you or your employer to even "put in motion a plan" which might result in not paying Social Security taxes, the Social Security Administration persists in its use of the term "contributions."

There is no clearer test of the attitude your government has toward your ability to reason than the "contributions" farce it continues. In the publications of the Social Security Administration, addressed to you, part of your pay is "contributions set aside for your future." In the law books of the U.S. Justice Department, addressed to federal prosecutors, that same money is "taxes due the Internal Revenue Service" which if intentionally unpaid would result in your being arrested.

The difference is quite clear to Pennsylvania Amish farmer Valentine Byler. Byler asked his government to exclude him from Social Security "contributions," since his Amish beliefs would prevent him from accepting a benefit check. Byler pointed out that he could much better "insure the future" of his family if the government stopped confiscating money which religious law would prevent Byler from getting back later.

But the Social Security Administration missed Byler's point and instead directed the Internal Revenue Service "to collect all the tax due."

Thus on May 1, in New Castle, Pennsylvania, one of the most revealing events in the forty-year history of the United States Social Security system took place. Three of Valentine Byler's Belgian mare workhorses were forcibly removed from his farm by agents of the district collection manager for the Internal Revenue Service to be sold at public auction.

As Byler had repeatedly made the federal agents aware, he was unable to replace the horses with farm machinery since his religion (and that of other Amish farmers in the same county) would forbid their use. The selling of the horses would cripple Byler's farm. The sale brought the government $460 which was applied to Valentine Byler's tax bill.

In spite of the Social Security Administration's publishing efforts to the contrary, the farmers in the rural county surrounding New Castle, Pennsylvania, now know what their government means by "contributions."

In the hands of the bureaucratic wordsmiths, definitions are, as Ira Gershwin put it, "a sometime thing" which change with the rising needs of those using them. The word "pool" is another casualty of this phenomenon.

A "pool" of money, dictionaries seem to agree, is a sum equal to the amount various contributors put there—an elementary, almost childish, thought but still one which the government tampers with for its own use.

If I tell ten people that I have "pooled" their contributions of $10 each into a created account, those ten have the right to believe that the account now contains at least $100.

If the ten people later look at the balance of the account and find that it contains, say, $75 they have the right to call me a liar and certainly the right to conclude that while something happened to their money, it was not pooled.

Yet when nine out of ten American workers are told their money is being "pooled in special trust funds," they have one of two choices: they can either suspend their notions of the word "pool," or they can believe that "pool" means what it has always meant and thus accept the administration's false promise as to what happens to their money.

Who does the government think is listening when it tells us, on the one hand, that our Social Security "contributions" will certainly double during the five years between 1975 and 1980 (just as they doubled during the previous four years), "to be pooled in special trust funds," and, on the other hand, that those same "special trust funds" will be empty by 1980?

What is being described is the most unique pooling effect in the history of money—more and more will become less and less!

Obviously, there is no "pool" just as there are no trust funds. Both words remain in the Social Security lexicon not because they are true, but because they help foster the public notion that Social Security is like insurance with its premium pools and trust funds regulated to support the promises made.

Since the Social Security Administration can't or won't regulate itself, it must choose the right words. The only words left in the federal insurance myth we've been looking at are the words chosen to make us believe we actually own the money that is taken from our paychecks or that we have a "legal right" to the benefits we've been promised.

As in the previous examples, what the bureaucratic language sounds like is the opposite of what it means. We've seen what it means to have a payroll "pooled in special trust funds," but what is really meant by "special"? Are the accounts individual, as suggested by the booklet rhetoric "your wages are entered on *your* social security record throughout your working years"? Does the phrase "legally enforceable in the courts," as administration spokesman Wilbur Cohen has said many times of Social Security benefits, really mean we have the right to what Congress has promised? Will the Supreme Court make Congress keep its word?

The administration's language has been professionally designed to make you feel secure that all the foregoing questions are to be answered Yes. But the answer to all the questions is a shattering No—and the bureaucrats know it.

The question of establishing a truly individual Social Security account was decided thirty-five years ago by the United States Supreme Court in declaring the act constitutional:

"The proceeds of both the employee and employer taxes," said the Court, "are to be paid into the Treasury like other internal revenue generally, and are not earmarked in any way."

Within twenty-one months of this Supreme Court decision, the public relations arm of the Social Security Administration was telling the public that payroll deductions "are strictly accounted for and kept separate from the general funds in the U.S. Treasury."

The question of "ownership" of the money Americans put into Social Security Administration hands was settled years ago, though government booklets on the subject never admit that fact— so expensive to you.

When the Social Security Act was being debated in the U.S. Congress in 1935, the framers considered certain aspects of the pending legislation "absolutely essential to fairness," as the June 12, 1935 issue of the *Congressional Record* noted.

"We can't ask support for a plan not at least as good as any American could buy from a private insurance company," said the report of the House Subcommittee for Finance. "The very least a citizen should expect is to get his money back upon retirement."

Fair enough. Thus when Social Security was established, American workers "owned" the money they gave in taxes. The original law guaranteed this in two critical ways.

If a taxpayer became sixty-five, the 1935 Congress decided, having paid into the system, but not having qualified for benefits for some reason, he would get back any money he paid in.

On the other hand, if a fully qualified taxpayer died before reaching sixty-five, a sum equal to all he paid in was to be given to his estate. These rules, Congress reasoned, simply established the obvious—that no one had to feel he was taking a chance "investing" with the federal government. Americans owned their future—for a while.

In 1939, with applications for refunds piling up, the federal government took another look at the guarantee it had issued. If the refunds were paid, it would cost millions from the mounting "trust account" which, though contrived, was of major interest to Americans still reeling from bank failures.

It took one legislative stroke that year to undo what one New York representative called "our first mistake," and with that single amendment the real nature of the government's promise to you began to take shape.

The 1939 law canceled the promised refunds. Those waiting for refund checks got instead a form letter telling of the amendment and how it would make the system more solvent.

The American citizens holding form letters instead of cash had not been waiting for a combination of their employers' share and their own, or even for any interest on the money the system had taken, only for what the Congress had made clear was "the least they should expect"—their own money back.

Today the only remnant of the 1935 promise is the hollow assurance, still rattling out of the U.S. Government Printing Office presses, that your Social Security card is "proof of your insurance policy with the government."

But how can a thing be "yours" if you can't control it? That's supposed to be the most basic element of ownership under law. Compare real ownership with the federal handling of "your insurance policy."

When a worker covered under Social Security dies, no money is paid to anyone. The government must first decide whether the worker left "dependents" under the federal definition. Though you might choose to leave the face value of "your insurance policy with the government" to your wife or your children, brother, sister, or even a favorite charity, the government has the right, under law, to ignore your wishes and pay no one at all.

Though the male worker might plan to leave benefits to his

wife, should he die, Social Security law says that merely being a wife isn't enough. The woman the worker leaves behind must be "caring for his dependent children" to qualify for a monthly death benefit. If the couple's children are grown or if the couple never had any children, the worker has earned the right to leave his wife a $255 burial fee—along with the government's best wishes.

As for the other beneficiaries a covered worker might have chosen on whom to bestow his death benefits (grown children, brother, sister, parent, charity, etc.), the Social Security Administration sends its regrets, but all would be refused. Ownership, under Social Security, turns out to be a very limited arrangement.

If Social Security's death-benefit "ownership" rules seem like a grotesque joke, consider how difficult the system makes it to "own" your retirement benefits.

From the signing of the Social Security Act, more and more worker taxes have been required to qualify for any retirement benefit at all. Today all American workers under forty-six must pay at least ten years' worth of tax to the Social Security Administration for the right to *any* retirement benefit. If you fall as much as three months short of this time, you get no benefit at retirement. Whatever tax was paid by you and your employer is lost. Remember, the 1935 money-back guarantee was "amended."

Thus, a worker beginning to pay taxes this year on a salary of $14,000 annually could, along with his employer, pay as much as $17,417 during the next nine years and not qualify for any retirement benefits.

If, at age thirty-five, he put this much in even the most conservative savings-and-loan he would find himself at age sixty-five with two options: either he could take $75,275 in cash to use any way he wants, or he could buy a contract entitling him to $560 a month for the rest of his life. Such are the differences between owning the money you pay and having it promised to you by a group with the right to "amend" their promise later.

The fact is that none of what the Social Security Administration has promised the American worker can be taken for granted.

No matter how high-sounding the promises of the "full faith and trust of the United States government" seem to be, Congress owes you nothing for your money. The Supreme Court decided the issue once and for all in 1956.

Ephraim Nestor was a naturalized American citizen who lived in the United States for forty-three years, twenty of which he and his employer paid taxes into the Social Security system. In 1956, during the American "red scare," Nestor was deported after he admitted being a member of the Communist party between the years 1933 and 1939.

Compounding the treatment, the U.S. government informed Nestor's wife, who had remained in this country, that deported Communists were not entitled to Social Security benefits, so she would get no further checks.

In the lawsuit that followed, Mrs. Nestor's lawyers argued not that Communists should get Social Security payments, but that the government had implied that workers covered by Social Security had "accrued property rights" to their money simply because they had paid.

The United States Supreme Court decided in favor of the government, and were candid in announcing that the case had nothing whatever to do with the rights of Communists. Congress, the Court said, had the right to take away benefits from anyone.

The majority opinion, written by Justice Harlan, was addressed to every American citizen when it said: "To engraft upon the Social Security System a concept of 'accrued property rights' would deprive it of the flexibility and boldness in adjustment to ever-changing conditions which it demands."

Today's American worker, as well as those retired on Social Security pensions, would do well to remind themselves of the 1956 Supreme Court decision. Among the "ever-changing conditions" the Court gives Congress the right to compensate for is the fact that the Social Security trust funds will be empty as early as 1980.

When Mr. Justice Black wrote the dissenting opinion in the

Nestor case, he knew the issue was more than communism. He was talking about your ability to count on your own future:

> The Court consoles those whose insurance is taken away today [wrote Justice Black], and others who may suffer the same fate in the future, by saying that a decision requiring the Social Security system to keep faith would "deprive it of the flexibility and boldness in adjustment to ever-changing conditions which it demands." People who pay premiums for insurance usually think they are paying for insurance, not for "flexibility and boldness." I cannot believe that any private insurance company in America would be permitted to repudiate its matured contracts with its policyholders who have regularly paid all their premiums in reliance upon the good faith of the company.

Justice Black warned every American to listen to how badly the federal promise had eroded by the words in the Court's decision:

> . . . they simply tell the contributors to this insurance fund [said Justice Black] that despite their own and their employers' payment to the Government, in paying the beneficiaries out of the fund, [it] is merely giving them something for nothing and can stop doing so when it pleases.

What, then, do Social Security defenders like Wilbur Cohen mean when they assure us that our rights are backed by "legal recourse in the courts for payment"?

The meaning is that you should listen to bureaucrats very carefully or you'll miss what they're telling you. The phrase "legal recourse in the courts for payment" means only that Congress must deal with each of us fairly in dividing up those benefits they choose to pay each year. The phrase means nothing that would hold one Congress to paying a level of benefits promised by a previous Congress. The Supreme Court says so.

It's very much like your father telling you and your brother that whenever he brings home candy he will divide it fairly between the two of you. But that if he doesn't want to, he won't bring home any candy at all. This gives him the right to say he will always deal fairly with you, but if you and your brother are smart you learn not to expect a treat.

The Supreme Court said it much more clearly thirty years ago than any Social Security Administration official has been willing to admit since:

> The benefits under Title II (Social Security Act) are like pensions, to be given or withheld in the discretion of Congress.

PART II

The Four Great Myths

*(and how we'd better learn
what they are or go broke)*

Up to now we have confined our discussion to what the federal government wants us to believe about Social Security. The Social Security Administration has the biggest "public information" staff within the biggest cabinet department (Health, Education, Welfare) in government and, as we've seen, most of what Americans know about Social Security is wrong and most of that wrong information is published by the administration.

But how about what the bureaucrats themselves believe? Governments are as likely as any other part of society to accept that what seems to be true is true and that, if enough other people believe, it will come to pass.

Remember that Social Security is a promise and, like all promises, it has at least three parts. There is what the promiser wants you to believe, what the promiser himself believes, and finally what is true in the end. The dismal truth for today's generation of working Americans is that as extravagant as the Social Security promise sounds, we can do better for ourselves. So much better, in fact, that if most Americans understood the facts of financial promises the Social Security system would collapse.

There are two iron-clad reasons to be certain that you can provide better for yourself and your family than the federal government can offer. First, the gaudy benefit growth figures the administration speaks of ($1,189-per-month retirement benefits in the year 2000) are not made possible by future governmental efficiency, but by more and more taxes used just as inefficiently as they are now. Second, the government is basing its promise (your future) on four fiscal "rules" which are simply false, as we'll see.

Beginning with the next chapter, we'll discuss how the Social Security Administration uses your money so poorly that you could do at least twice as well for yourself without any financial background.

For now, it's important we understand that the present Social Security system cannot continue—that its principles are so false and expensive that the scheme will soon be crushed in its own weight.

Let's take a look at the four supposed facts upon which the government is willing to stake your future security.

3] Myth 1: *"Social Security benefits are inflation-proof."*

One of the enduring marvels of the government dialogue with the public is the ability of the bureaucrat to ignore what doesn't fit his argument while taking credit for what the taxpayer himself provides.

In late 1972 when a provision was added to the Social Security Act to link both payroll taxes and benefits to "an automatic increase plan," administration officials couldn't wait to label Social Security "inflation-proof."

During 1973 thirty-two separate press releases from the Baltimore information office of the Social Security Administration contained a reference to the system's "inflation-proof" benefits. Interestingly, during that same year only four official mentions were made of the fact that taxes must be hiked in every year benefits go up.

"The beauty of the present program is that there is no need for the retiree to worry about inflation," says University of Georgia Professor Richard E. Johnson, whose 1974 defense of the system became the official administration reply to calls for reform.

"Today," proclaims Professor Johnson, "an automatic provision of the Act increases benefits as the cost of living increases. No commercial insurance contract can provide that benefit."

Former Secretary of Health, Education, and Welfare Wilbur E. Cohen has stated repeatedly, "The Social Security plan now guarantees an inflation-proof benefit."

We had better learn to recognize this for the massive con game it is. Rather than being "inflation-proof," today's system is virtually guaranteed to produce inflation and, more than other future governmental commitment, fuel its fire.

The reason is as simple as understanding what inflation is. Though many economic and social theories exist on what causes inflation, there is agreement on what the condition actually is. Inflation is too much currency in supply in relation to the goods or services available.

Thus, as long as the Social Security system was content to take one worker's tax dollars and give them to someone else, the system did not create the need for new dollars. Taking money from one pocket to put the same amount in another pocket may not be "insurance," as the government claims, but at least it was all being done with the same money.

But the Congress has not been content with the pocket-to-pocket theory for some time. For the last twenty years the system has been undergoing a redesign which compels the present working generation to pay heavily for the promises made to the last working generation. The labels have all stayed the same—a governmental insurance plan backed by vast reserves—but the reality changed.

Making more and more extravagant claims every election year puts senior congressmen back at their committee posts, but it doesn't explain where the money is coming from. It was being taken from trust funds, which no longer deserve the name, with the hope that the current working generation wouldn't notice what was really happening to them.

There was no need to consider who gets the bill—today's

worker—as long as we weren't asking questions. We watched the reserves balance evaporate at the same time the Social Security tax doubled (between the years 1970 and 1974) without making Social Security an issue in a single major election, so the signal to Washington was pretty clear. If we believed this plan could "insure our future" we'd believe anything.

But reality is, after all, reality, and even the dimmest government actuary could see that the financial well was running dry. The last two years of Social Security payouts totaled 47 percent more than were in the limping trust accounts, and by 1977, at the latest, the combined totals of forty-year-old reserves and payroll taxes, tripled since 1966, won't be enough.

The 1974 Social Security trustees' report concludes, ". . . it is certain that additional income to the cash benefits program or some adjustment in the benefit structure will be needed eventually."

Get ready. The language is beginning to clear up. The trustees as well as top administration officials are looking for ways to announce that "additional income to the cash benefits program" means money from the general treasury—income tax money.

With the first dollar paid in Social Security benefits that does not come from Social Security taxes or trust funds, all pretense of a noninflationary Social Security system ends. That first dollar is "new" money to be followed by billions more. Even those Social Security Administration officials who refuse to admit the trust funds will be gone by 1980 (Commissioner James Cardwell is one) acknowledge that the true deficit will reach $20 billion during the 1980s.

What could be a more perfect tactic than to label the bail-out plan, for twenty years of raiding the treasury, as making the Social Security system "inflation-proof"?

Nobody laughs when men like Wilbur J. Cohen, who developed the present system, or Professor Richard E. Johnson, currently trying to defend it, call the "automatic provision" of benefit increases something "no commercial insurance contract can provide."

Such chattering by these two is obscene. Both are aware that, under law, none of the so-called automatic benefit increases can take place unless taxes are raised to meet them during the same year. Both also admit freely that those retired are not paying for their own benefits, but are receiving them from present workers who allow themselves to be taxed on the hope that the next generation will do the same. It is absurd to say that no private insurance can do the same.

Once you agree to pay the insurance premiums for someone else, any insurance company on earth would gladly offer to raise the benefits to that person—in any year you're willing to raise your premium payment.

Calling a corrupted, improbable set of promises no longer able to pay for themselves an inflation-proof plan for the future is classic bureaucratic double-talk but, in many ways, an excellent public relations ploy.

Consider what has happened. Congress and the Social Security Administration look at a plan, doomed to deficits during years of covering up impossible pledges by reducing the trust balance, and decide that disaster can be put off for a while by "automatically" raising benefits to meet the cost of living. Taxes, says the administration, will also rise. But tax levels won't be tied to the cost of living. They will rise "automatically" with the average wage, which traditionally rises faster than the cost-of-living index.

The plan doesn't solve the basic funding problem of Social Security, as the trustees' own future deficit figures show, but it does accomplish two important things. Thirty million beneficiary-voters are kept happy with Social Security checks that seem to be getting better. And Congress can escape all further blame for Social Security tax hikes because they will be "automatic"—announced by computers instead of congressmen.

4] Myth 2: *"Social Security doesn't need normal reserves."*

Living as he does in an "anything we do is right" universe, the bureaucrat allows himself marvelous free reign with normal reason. He can, for instance, whimsically rule that certain pesty parts of the truth don't apply to him or his associates. By invoking this rule the federal government justifies demanding a strict reserves system for the private insurance industry but not for its own Social Security Administration.

The reason for this seeming inconsistency, say Social Security trustees, is quite simple. Private insurance companies cannot count on convincing new customers to buy insurance policies every year, while the Social Security Administration can. The trustees point with seeming pride to the fact that the United States is a "closed shop" when it comes to "selling" new federal insurance. Nine out of every ten new members of the American work force have no choice but to accept a Social Security policy. It comes down to a matter of faith in one's sales force. The bureaucrats exhibit less faith in an army of salespeople selling their product than they do in

IRS investigators backed by federal attorneys, guns, and jails—a tough point to argue.

Thus during 1974 the private life insurance industry took in premiums of slightly more than $50 billion while the Social Security Administration collected taxes of $59 billion. However, while various combinations of state laws and fiscal prudence compelled private life insurance companies to add to existing reserves by over $12 billion (25 percent of what they collected), Social Security added to its reserves by $90 million (less than 1 percent of tax collections).

Obviously the Social Security Administration is depending quite a lot on "compulsion" as making a pretty big difference in the way one needs to keep one's books. To see if they're right, we need to know a little more about why we insist that private insurance have adequate reserves.

Simply stated, tough reserve rules for private insurance warn the industry they have no right to tell the public, "We're willing to bet your insurance coverage that we'll have a good year." They must instead have assets enough to guarantee coverage.

It works this way: If you have a life insurance business with a fairly average collection of risks as customers, you can be statistically certain that less than 60 percent of your premium income will be needed to pay benefits in a given year and less than 10 percent to pay your sales force. That leaves a pretty good chunk left over. You can either spend the surplus on whatever you like, or put it in reserve. As long as you keep selling more policies one year than you did the year before, the averages say you'll never need the surplus. So why bother with a reserve account? Have a ball!

But there's a catch. The first year that you don't sell more than the year before, or are forced to take on bigger risks to do so, or suffer any of the myriad business conditions that make for a bad year, the whole pyramid you've built begins falling on your head. Without reserves your customers are never insured by anything but your hopes. The government quite properly says your hopes aren't enough. Enough liquid assets must be available, say state regulations, so that each policyholder is protected no matter how many other policies are sold or not sold.

The federal government has decided that since "compulsory social insurance is assured of continuing income [new workers must come into the program], it does not have to build up the kind of reserves" a private company needs. The Social Security trustees have stated in many reports that they, unlike private enterprise planners, can count on "current income meeting current obligations." That's part of your income they're talking about "count[ing] on," so you had better be aware of why they feel so sure.

Can the federal government be certain that its ability to compel new workers to pay is enough to abandon a true reserve system —in fact to foresee, in the 1974 annual report, no reserve at all?

Samuel R. Burkett, president of the American Association of Actuaries, believes it is not.

A safe reserve [says Burkett], is more than just a substitute for future sales. It is the financial shield against all manner of unknown disaster whether fiscal or physical. No individual policy, public or private, is genuinely safe without a reserve unless someone within the system can guarantee to foretell the future.

What all of this means is that the bureaucrats have banked too much on "compulsion" to make up for two decades of bookkeeping folly. The so-called guarantee of a "good next year," as implied by the power of the government to "cover" the new worker with its system, is not enough to secure your future or the future of Social Security.

Because the U.S. Congress and the Social Security Administration long ago decided to abandon insurance economics in favor of a pay-as-we-go system, the concept of a "good next year" is not quite the same as in private industry.

American Social Security needs a stable economy to be able to balance its tricky month-to-month budgets. A limited (or nonexistent) reserve system needs a climbing birthrate to be sure enough workers will be on the job in the future to make good on the promises with their pay. By the same token, full employment is a must.

Where does this leave our Social Security system which, we're told, relies so heavily on compulsion? Nowhere unless some federal administrator can figure out how to compel a slowing of world inflation, or compel American couples to have as many children as they used to, or use compulsion to beat unemployment.

One alternative, of course, is to make better predictions. But Social Security makes notoriously bad predictions.

In at least one press release each year, the Social Security Administration points with pride to the fact that it does not "rely" upon other governmental agencies to make its predictions on birthrate or inflation—the two most important elements to its pay-as-we-go future funding system. This self-reliance may explain why the last decade of administration predictions have been so dismally wrong.

For the past ten years the Social Security's Office of the Actuary has used its own "future population projection" instead of the models offered by the Bureau of the Census or the United States Public Health Service, each of which showed a declining U.S. birthrate. Thus for the years 1965 through 1975 the Social Security Administration overestimated the population of future American workers by a whopping 33 percent. In a continued regard for its own opinion which would embarrass Chicken Little, the latest (1974) Social Security Administration estimate of U.S. birthrate shows a long-term rise. In fact the U.S. Census Bureau maintains a log showing a decline in our birthrate to a true zero population growth during the 1980s. We can only expect that the administration's estimates will go further astray.

Since a nonreserve insurance system depends upon knowing how many will be on hand in a given year to share the benefit load, we can expect more surprises in the future concerning what our tax share will actually be. In 1971 for instance, the Social Security Administration's forecasters expected a 1974 tax base of $12,000 rising to $12,800 by 1975. As our paychecks showed, the real figures were $13,200 for 1974 and $14,100 for 1975—a 10 percent error each year.

The errors are not all due to inferior population planning. Some were caused when Congress approved cost-of-living increases in benefit levels not expected by the Social Security Administration. One of the reasons the increases were not expected is that during the last decade the Social Security Administration overestimated American gains in real wages (pay increases less inflation) by more than 29 percent. They continue this strangely founded faith by basing benefit promises to today's workers on the theory that real wages will grow an average of 2 percent every year between now and the end of the century. The U.S. Labor Department, whose real-wage studies are published monthly, shows a decline in paycheck buying power over the last three years, ending 1974. For today's wage earner a continuation of these kinds of statistical "problems" will mean more unpleasant surprises in the FICA box of future paychecks.

It is not the purpose here to charge our government for not being infallible. The most renowned economists in the world fail in complex predictions regularly. Rather, the blame lies in the creation of a situation in which a mistake is paid for not by those who made it, but by those forced to rely upon another's judgment. The holders of contracts with adequately funded and regulated insurance, pension, or annuity companies aren't blessed with infallible administrators handling their cash, but they are reasonably certain that they will get what has been promised in spite of a changing economy.

For now things have gone too far. The funds on hand and predicted for the future cannot withstand the consequences of the planning mistakes already made by the Social Security Administration and its congressional planners.

Bureaucrats willing to give away more than they were willing to tax have created an unfundable burden. Where in 1947 one out of every seventy-one Americans received Social Security benefits, today one in every seven collects. By 1990 the ratio is expected to worsen to one benefits recipient for every six Americans.

Though Social Security Administration birthrate analysts have seemed not to notice, we are producing more beneficiaries than we are people to pay the bills. In 1955 seven U.S. workers paid taxes for every person collecting benefits. Today fewer than three workers "pool" their "contributions" for each Social Security beneficiary. By early next century only two Americans will be working for every one collecting a check.

When the 1974 Social Security trustees' report speaks of the certainty "that additional income to the cash benefits program or some adjustment in the benefit structure will be needed," they mean past predictions have been so far off that if we don't agree to higher taxes they can't keep their benefit promises.

With each new annual "adjustment" from the predicted level of Social Security taxes (previously announced levels of Social Security tax have been wrong in each of the last five years), Social Security Administration officials cite unpredictable "economic factors" as the excuse. This will also no doubt be the reason given when the first benefit "adjustments" are announced. It will somehow be our own fault for being factors in an unpredictable economy.

Social Security's administrators have bet our reserves and lost. Now they must hope we won't notice. If we don't we'll have to share the national shame. When the bureaucrats speak of unpredictable economies, they must be answered by an electorate that knows it's been cheated. Why were they willing to make promises based on factors they knew they couldn't control? Couldn't they see that the compulsion they relied on so heavily would not insure lowered inflation or full employment? How could they make benefit promises based on a rising birthrate when they could see it was falling?

One ugly truth remains. When the Social Security innovators who gave us the "we-don't-need-normal-reserves" concept allowed the guarantee to disappear, they also took away our option to object. They knew very well that an insurance plan without reserves has no options. There can be no tolerance for allowing those who feel cheated to leave the system.

Thus when Social Security Commissioner James B. Cardwell said in a 1974 interview that making the system optional to the young worker "would impair benefits promised to those retired," the inference was that those dropping out would be letting down the retired generation. The fact is that the present hand-to-mouth budgeting hodge-podge couldn't be made optional no matter how obviously bad it has become. Rather than its fictional image of a system "adjusting automatically to inflation," Social Security is an insatiable money consumer which will need more and more cash just to keep its deficits from growing faster than its benefits.

We need only keep in mind a single fact to answer the inane bureaucratic notion of a no-reserve fund with the legal right to compel new members. Social Security cannot withstand the truth. We don't have the option to drop our "coverage" because the slightest exercise of that option (by as little as 10 percent of the workforce) would destroy the system. By contrast, a normally funded and regulated true insurance system could be dropped by nine out of ten of its policyholders without endangering at all the benefits of any who remain. Social Security retains its compulsive hold on your paycheck because it couldn't exist without it for even a year.

5] Myth 3: *"Social Security encourages savings."*

Of all the paternalistic slogans fostered by the architects and present administrators of Social Security, none is more amazing than the fancy that the system encourages saving. To accept this requires an almost surreal disfiguring of the facts.

In a 1973 survey taken by the New York Times Company, some 62 percent of those questioned in a national sample agreed that "Social Security tends to encourage saving," though no other question in the study was designed to discover why the belief exists.

The official version of this idea is explained regularly in at least four Social Security Administration booklets wherein we are told "social security benefits are designed to establish a basic floor of retirement, death benefit, or disability income which encourages family savings to supplement it."

Here we embark on another one of those "bad-is-really-good" government explanations of the facts. "Social Security benefits," we are told, "are intended to replace part of the family income lost through death, disability or retirement of the wage earner." The implication is, of course, that replacing "part" of one's income is good and that we really shouldn't expect any more. In fact, the government tells us, the gap between what a family needs in replaced income and what Social Security pays is "intended in the program" to "encourage family savings." Presumably, then, if the gap between lost wages and benefits were wider we would be "encouraged" to save even more. Few other organizations would dare use as a selling point the fact that their service will not do all of what you'd like.

The key to all the bureaucrats' shadowy logic is whether the American worker pays for a "partial protection" program or whether he should expect that his mounting Social Security tax bills underwrite full protection for his current income and retirement.

It is a simple economic truth that the "pass-through" system used by Social Security to take from some to give to others (while charging an administrator's fee on top) is the least efficient way to use money.

Almost any other method of handling the current $60 billion per year in Social Security taxes would result in more benefits paid to more people or a lower tax for all. Even the simplest efficiencies applied to Social Security funds would double their value to most taxpayers. This difference in value is so vast that the current system amounts to a fraud, as we'll see in later chapters. For now we should examine the peculiar bureaucratic conviction that impounding more than 11 percent of the American payroll somehow makes it easier for us to save.

Since more than 68 cents of every dollar we are compelled to pay in Social Security tax is intended for retirement benefits, the system is chiefly an enforced savings plan. If compulsory saving is supposed to "encourage" voluntary saving, as the government contends, then we should see a relationship between Social Security taxation and the amount the average American family can save on its own. There is a relationship and it's quite interesting.

During the early days of Social Security payroll deductions

(between the years 1937 and 1949), when only 2 percent of the American payroll could be taxed, the most that an individual wage earner and his employer could pay was $60 per year.

In the last of these relatively low taxation years, 1949, the average American family had amassed savings of $241. From now on, when the term "savings" is used the meaning is to be "the amount of money left, after all tax deductions and living expenses have been met, which a family can afford to place in a bank, savings and loan, credit union account or similar savings outlet."

The $241 that a typical 1949-vintage American family had put away was of course a purely voluntary fund. By the same token, this savings account was for more than simply retirement accumulation. Just as families plan today, savings covered major-appliance purchases, vacations, and emergencies as well as retirement.

Which brings us to a discussion of the level of compulsory savings which can be imposed on a nation's families before the encouragement to save is completely eroded. Obviously, if a government's enforced pension savings plan equals, during a single year, a significant percentage of what a family has accumulated, for all savings purposes, during a lifetime, the savings incentive dies.

Looked at in this way, the $1.67 billion in Social Security tax collected in 1949 from American payrolls represents an average of $41 in tax for each family. Thus the tax level in that year equaled 17 percent of what an average family had accumulated on its own.*

By 1955 American savings had grown from $241 per family to $377—a 56 percent advance managing to stay slightly ahead of the post-Korean War inflation. But the family share of Social Security tax had risen from $41 to $136—a sobering 230 percent rise. Social Security taxes in 1955 had become 36 percent of total American savings.

* Though the percentage of American households covered by Social Security has grown since 1949 to its present 90 percent level, the figures in this study have been equalized statistically for the years mentioned.

In 1965 "the little tax to build a floor of security" was swirling upward into a financial storm. The $168 maximum tax for 1955 had become the $348 1965 model—an increase of 208 percent. Though family savings in 1965 had swelled to a $594 average, the payroll share of Social Security tax had leaped 246 percent to $335 per family. One year of the government's enforced savings taxation now equaled 56 percent of all the nation's personal accumulation of funds.

Still the tax that was supposed to help Americans save grew faster than Americans could save. By the end of 1969, though the country's savings had grown each quarter of the year, the Social Security tax grew more. The 47 percent gain in national savings (to $877 per family) was more than wiped out by the 85 percent hike in family Social Security taxes since 1965. The $31.5 billion 1969 Social Security tax bill equaled 70 percent of our savings. And the worst was coming.

The 1972 Social Security tax rolled over U.S. savings gains by a wide margin. While American families were logging their third straight year of over-$1,000 bank accounts, the government took $4.5 billion more from payrolls. With more ground lost, Americans in 1972 found that the family federal insurance bill for a single year equaled 79 percent of their life savings.

There is no reason whatever to believe that taxes encourage saving when the tax grows faster than the nest egg. If any doubt of this principle lingered, it died in 1974 when American savings skidded to a halt.

Between 1969 and early 1973 the American family seemed to have battled mounting inflation to a standstill. There were flurries of bank withdrawals in 1971 and 1972, but overall the four-year period saw an 87 percent jump in family savings.

As the cost-of-living index rose in 1973 by nearly 12 percent, the regular 10 to 15 percent leap in Social Security tax further gouged take-home pay until savings became more an act of fear than a decision of wealth.

The savings gains of 1973 were the greatest in a decade, but unlike previous years spending didn't keep pace. The $1,202 average family bank account in the beginning of 1973 swelled to $1,644 by the year's end. But retail sales figures for the year show that banks were filling up with money we were afraid to spend. In 1974 the fears became real.

In no year in history did Americans take more out of their savings than in 1974. By March of 1974 the $1,644 bank account of Christmas 1973 had shrunk to $1,517. In June the average family savings balance had slipped to $1,286, and by September to $1,161. At the end of the year American savings (then $1,055) was in danger of falling below the thousand-dollar level for the first time since 1969. More than $26 billion was drained in a single year. All of the savings gains American families had made in the previous five years had been wiped out.

But Social Security tax increases did not stop in 1974; they were headed for a grim milestone. A second year of double-digit raises in the cost of living meant Americans were forced to spend more than their take-home pay just to keep even. Rising still faster than inflation, Social Security taxes were hiked another 14 percent to nearly $60 billion.

Thus in 1974, with savings dwindling and Social Security setting another spending record, the payroll tax bill for the year equaled a mind-bending 99.3 percent of everything American families had saved during their lives.

Since no long-term halt in the savings withdrawal trend is expected, 1975 should end all notions of a "tax to help us save" as a 1971 Social Security Administration booklet called the program. For the first time one single annual Social Security tax bill will be more than all the life savings of every family in the United States.

At the same time Social Security Administration spokesmen see a connection between the current American plight and their own activities. "Social Security," said Wilbur Cohen in 1974, "gives individuals an incentive to save and work to improve their economic security." This is something like saying floods encourage people to learn swimming.

Certainly wholesale confiscation of payroll doesn't make it easier to keep more take-home pay for savings, as the government would like us to believe. But what about the other side of the coin? Does Social Security, in fact, make it less likely that we'll save? There is growing evidence that it does.

Research conducted during 1973–74, in part by Harvard University economist Martin Feldstein under the sponsorship of the National Science Foundation, indicates that Social Security "depresses personal saving by 30 to 50 percent."

"The implication that social security halves the rate of personal saving," says Feldstein, "is startling but not unreasonable. For middle and low-income families, social security is a complete substitute for a substantial rate of private savings."

Nor is the private savings account merely an abstract element in a general picture of economics. It is well known that where personal savings is inhibited, general economic hardship soon follows throughout the system.

The Feldstein study also indicates the direct effect of a reduction in personal savings to a decrease in private capital stock. "A 38 percent reduction in private savings," says Feldstein, "would also decrease private capital stock by the same amount. This decrease implies a substantial reduction in Gross National Product."

Another 1974 study of Social Security, conducted by Robert S. Kaplan of Carnegie–Mellon University and Roman L. Weil of the Georgia Institute of Technology, includes the following about the system's effect upon saving and that effect upon the nation.

Old Age Survivors Insurance (OASI) benefits are a partial replacement for retirement savings and insurance. Therefore, people entitled to OASI benefits save less and consume more than they would in the absence of a federal program. If the federal program is financed on a pay-as-you-go basis, there is no savings at the federal level either. Therefore, as an OASI program expands, there may be less overall saving and, hence, less capital accumulation in the economy as a whole. This will affect the future productivity of the nation's capital stock and the future costs of the OASI program since such capital accumulation is, at least, partially responsible for gains in future productivity and, hence, real wages. To the extent that the OASI program is currently inhibiting savings and capital accumulation, we may have additional problems in maintaining recent levels of real wage growth.

Throughout 1974 real growth did fall, of course, as did the level of Gross National Product—the best recognized indicator of economic recession. Though no single government policy can be responsible for all our financial ills, some certainties do emerge. Rather than providing any savings "encouragement" whatever, Social Security seems to play a major part in undermining the economic system that pays the benefits.

6] Myth 4: *"Social problems can be treated if we allocate as much money for them as we do for national defense."*

Americans have bought themselves too much government. We have not only accepted the idea that governments can solve problems, but that big government should be entrusted with the biggest problems. This can be a very comforting idea to hold. Since government continues to grow, holders of the big-is-better theory can believe that things are improving.

With a sincere desire to solve social problems, Americans have become the most insatiable consumers of government programs in the history of the world. During the 1930s, with economic depression gripping nearly all the world's industrial nations, the United States put in motion an expansion of federal bureaucracy without parallel in the past. The momentum thus begun was to give Americans during the next forty-five years: a 330 percent rise in the number of federal agencies, congressional committees and subcommittees; a better than 600 percent rise in the cost of federal government; and a national debt approaching the half-trillion mark —more than $2,450 for every man, woman, and child in the nation.

Though there is no denying that the vigorous expansion of government during the '30s and beyond filled a need for hope that made our depression years more bearable, one question remains: Does money spent by the federal government really solve social problems?

During the same years in which we mounted the largest single monetary assault on suffering the world had ever seen, the American economy faltered, our economic influence diminished, and the dollar fell from the symbol of strength it was to barely the fourth or fifth most desired currency on world markets.

During these years the total number of American families living at official poverty levels decreased less than 15 percent in terms of national population.

The question remains: Did we buy less suffering with our depletion of resources or simply more government? Governments do not have money of their own, so their choices have certain limitations. To the extent that government choices about money increase, individual money choices by citizens decrease. Somehow, during the last forty-five years, Americans have consistently allowed their choices to disappear.

And with all this a curious rallying cry has developed. We can mobilize a real campaign against poverty, say some social planners, if we only go at it with the same vigor as the Pentagon generals do their campaigns. After all, they say time and again, shouldn't we at least devote the same energy and resources to improving life as we do to systematically snuffing it out?

The guns-*vs.*-mercy approach seems to have a unique and compelling effect on our national morality. It is as though we have come to accept that military victory carries with it a blot of social stigma that must be erased no matter what the cost. As a lobbying technique in raising money for social projects, the same appeal is used constantly.

Thus when Princeton University Dean Emeritus J. Douglas Brown testified before the Senate Special Committee on Aging in

1973 his plea for additional funds for Medicare was not confined simply to the merits of that project:

> It is most difficult to understand why, in a budget that assigns vast billions to the defense establishment, to space activities, and to many other large endeavors here and abroad, there is need to withdraw from the old and the sick a hundred dollars here and two hundred there when they need help most.

Nor was then President Lyndon Johnson unaware of the tested bromide when he appealed to Congress, in a 1967 request for an increase in the Social Security program, that they be part of a nation "as dedicated to spending the necessary small sums to help the poor as we are to spending millions on destruction."

A 1974 survey taken by the National Broadcasting Company indicated that the majority of Americans believe the biggest reason their country "can't do more about domestic problems" is "runaway defense spending."

It is certainly not the purpose of this book to advocate unchecked military spending, which is already at devastating levels throughout the world, nor to begrudge even a single dollar spent to alleviate suffering. What must be understood is that giving money to the federal government is not the same as solving a social problem. In fact, where spending such money creates the false impression that social problems are being solved, the money could hardly be worse spent.

The fact is that this nation allows much more economic hardship than is necessary because the money which we allocate to solve problems is spent so inefficiently. To combine the natural ineffectiveness of government spending with the misguided notion that we under-finance social programs in favor of bombs creates an almost hopeless situation for our poor; we are guaranteeing to continue spending more money in ways that will not reach them.

It is simply not true that our social programs want for money that is going to the Pentagon. If there is a military establishment in

this country (no one doubts there is), then the welfare establishment is bigger, better paid, and better able to extract tax dollars on
the promise of "security" always around the next monetary corner.

In 1967 this nation spent slightly more than $70 billion on
military projects while slightly less than $31 billion was spent in
the budget category called "income security." While "income
security" includes both federal public aid and Social Security programs, the great bulk of the money (more than 83 percent) goes to
the Social Security Administration. However these figures seem to
fuel the arguments of the social spenders, the fact is that both the
welfare establishment and the military establishment doubled their
budgets between 1960 and 1967.

The important story is what has happened since then. As
incredible as it may seem, the generals have been given a lesson in
spending. Between the years 1967 and 1970 the federal defense
budget rose from $70 billion to $80.3 billion—or 14½ percent.
During the same years the "income security" budget went from
$30 billion to $43.8 billion—or 42 percent. Again, even though
"income security" includes a number of other federal assistance
programs, Social Security increases account for more than 90 percent of the rise in this category.

Still the Pentagon had a sizable lead over the Social Security
Administration. But the lead was eroding. In only thirty-six months
"income security" had grown from being 44 percent of the U.S.
defense budget to more than 55 percent.

By 1971, as the American involvement in Southeast Asia
grew less and pressure from the Congress increased, the defense
budget was cut $2.6 billion to $77.7 billion. This reduction, bitterly
fought by Pentagon officials, came on top of a $900 million de-
crease the year before.

In that same year "income security" grew another 27 percent
to $55.7 billion. While Congress and many editorial writers com-
plained that the Pentagon budget had not been pared sharply
enough, federal income benefits quietly grew to 71 percent of total
American defense costs.

By 1973 it was clear that whatever federal assistance lobby existed it was certainly stronger than the Pentagon lobby. While the military budget fell more than 5 percent between 1968 and 1973 (the budget was cut in three of the six years and allowed only inflationary increases in the other three), "income security" led by the Social Security Administration increased its budget by 123 percent during the same period.

During the infighting and economic adjustments of 1973 and 1974, the welfare and military establishments each made do with roughly $76 billion in American tax dollars.

For 1975, projections by the Senate Defense Appropriations Sub-Committee and the Social Security Administration indicate that the two-year-long stand-off between the agencies will be broken; for the first time in the nation's modern history *more* will be spent for "income security" than for national security.

To make possible this whirlwind of national refinancing, our welfare establishment accomplished what the Pentagon chiefs had never been able to do. The budget for one single department of government had been increased more than 332 percent between 1960 and 1974. This period in American history began with nearly half our federal tax dollars allocated for defense and less than 20 percent for income benefits. The score now stands at nearly 31 percent of U.S. taxes pledged to Social Security and 30 percent for defense spending.

Truly, the change in national priorities has been revolutionary —more than enough to offset the notion that we lack a commitment to help those in need equal to our megatonnage in destructive power. But what has been purchased? Since 1967, when President Johnson urged for the "necessary small sums" to bolster Social Security, we have spent more than $300 billion—equal to almost the entire national debt—in a nearly hopeless effort. The money could hardly have been used any more poorly.

In 1970 the average couple receiving Social Security retirement benefits was eligible to a combined check of $198.90 per month. By July of 1974 this combined benefit had risen to $310 per month. This 56 percent rise in benefits no doubt helped those who received it, but how much did it help?

Remember that during this same period the cost-of-living index rose nearly 32 points, meaning that the real increase in buying power for the average American retired couple was only 24 percent—averaging about 6 percent per year.

For the average individual receiving Social Security benefits, the years between 1970 and 1974 saw an increase in monthly benefits from $114 to $181 which, when adjusted for cost-of-living increases, raised his or her buying power less than 7 percent per year.

To accomplish this bit of betterment, the American working population and their employers saw their Social Security tax bill increase more than 68 percent (better than *twice* the cost-of-living rise), averaging 17 percent each year.

The lesson to be learned here is that voting money to help those in need (as the great majority of Social Security beneficiaries are) is not enough in itself. To spend so vast an amount of a nation's resources while accomplishing so little is criminal.

Since 1970 the maximum Social Security tax has increased more than 120 percent, dwarfing all other tax increases. Yet during this time the benefits paid to those we sought to help have averaged much less than official poverty levels. The average retired couple receives a total of $3,720 per year in Social Security payments while the typical single recipient "benefits" a meager $2,172 a year.

Keep in mind that our Social Security system is not a no-strings-attached award to those who receive checks. The law says that it is "an income replacement" to be reduced where other income is earned. Currently earnings of $200 per month are enough to reduce benefits to the tune of one dollar for each additional two dollars of income.

Thus, before the American working population congratulates itself on the profound tax sacrifices made to alleviate suffering, the true value of what those taxes bought must be considered.

In exchange for a tax bounty equal to a redeployment of the entire national debt, we have earned the right to say to a man or woman trying to live on $181 per month in Social Security that if he or she seeks to supplement this amount by even $50 a week in earnings the benefits will be reduced.

If the right to make that bargain, and others like it, seems worth $300 billion to us, then we can be sure that more administration advisers will make more speeches this year imploring us to spend more money in exactly the same way. If we still say nothing, we have agreed.

Since the American taxpayer has more than proved his willingness to be taxed for some social good, he should be rewarded with results. For $300 billion spent, today's retired, disabled, and dependent deserve much more. And today's working population deserve a far richer promise. Instead our Social Security recipients live in poverty while the Social Security Administration freely admits that each succeeding American working population will receive less per dollar taxed.*

It is not that $300 billion isn't enough to improve the quality of life in this country. Our sacrifices can't pay off because the taxes they produce are being used in the worst possible way—to do the job the Social Security trust funds were supposed to do but can do no longer.

Consider what the current American Social Security system is and it will be apparent why so much money has done so little. Using 1975 as an example, the Internal Revenue Service is charged with collecting Social Security payroll and self-employment taxes which, for the first time in the system's history, will not even be enough to pay all the mounting benefit bills for the year. Thus, all pretense of a "pooling of funds" into a trust account should be

---

* Even though today's beginning worker will pay four to five times the taxes his father paid, the Chief Actuary of the Social Security Administration estimates he will do 20 percent worse in tax-to-payoff ratio than his father—his own son will do 14 percent worse than that.

dropped. Instead, one month's taxes will be collected, Social Security Administration expenses will be deducted, and the remainder will be paid out immediately. To accomplish even this wheel-spinning bit of accounting, the administration will require an additional hand-out from the General Revenue Fund.

We would be challenged to concoct a more bankrupt method for one generation to help another. What would you think of a friend of yours who came to you with the following scheme to help out his mother? His idea is to deduct money from each of his paychecks and keep it in his mattress, and he has agreed to pay someone else 2 or 3 percent for the service of bringing the cash to his mother each month. Appallingly, this is what Social Security has become.

For the federal government to use our tax money so stupidly, while dubbing the whole process "insurance" and assuring the future of those who are forced to pay, amounts to the rankest kind of fraud.

Up to now we have been concerned only with the government's methods for concealing what has happened to American Social Security and the almost unbelievable short-sightedness which has brought us where we are.

From now on we will concentrate on the "generation of victims," today's workers, and the plan they are locked into. The difference between the value of what they pay and the value of what they are offered in exchange amounts to the largest-scale swindle in financial history.

7] "We've Got You Covered"

Whatever else can be said of the federal government's attempts at concealing what has become of the American Social Security system, one thing is certain: they are not unmotivated acts. There is something to hide. If you're working, you're paying too much and if you're retired, you're protected too little.

Today's Social Security is bad insurance (or no insurance at all) forced upon the American working population at fraudulently high rates at a time in the country's history when real protection is most needed. It is a plan whose only hope for success is that we don't realize what it is and how little it's worth.

The glittering promises of $2,000- and $3,000-a-month tax-free pensions offered to today's worker resemble most the prizes displayed at a carnival ring-toss game: They will either not be awarded or the "winner" will soon discover he paid more to be in the game than the prize is worth.

The game is being played against working Americans because it is their belief in the Social Security system that is its only true reserve. The trust funds can no longer guarantee Social Security nor will any of the system's internal assumptions hold it together. All that is left is the average working American's faith that Social Security gives him a fair shake—that his enormous social insurance tax bill somehow endows his future at a fair return.

When a $75-billion-a-year scheme is buttressed by faith alone, we can be certain that every institutional marketing technique available will be used to maintain that faith. Since the product is faulty, the sales pitch must be foolproof. The largest single federal money source is at stake.

The Great American Social Security Hoax continues, because, for the most part, we don't know how insurance works. When administration spokesmen say "Social Security is group insurance" which represents a "fair investment for American families," we believe that the 114 percent rise in Social Security taxes since 1971 is buying us that much more protection. When James B. Cardwell, as commissioner of the Social Security Administration, tells us that the system's costs make it "vastly more efficient than private insurance," we believe him. Both statements are catastrophically expensive lies.

Whenever the Social Security Administration is asked by some research organization, newspaper, or magazine to explain the system, cooperation by the largest public information staff in government (outside the Pentagon) comes swiftly. The answers are ready, we are told, because the American worker should "know the facts about Social Security."

Thus when the privately financed Research Institute of America and California Taxpayers' Lobby *Newsletter* sought Social Security information, during 1974 and 1975, for their readers and contributors, both were told of the hypothetical Richard Williams family and how well the family is protected by his Social Security contributions.

The family, according to the administration example, is headed by thirty-five-year-old Richard Williams, a salesman who has always paid the maximum Social Security tax. His wife, Mary, cares for the couple's two children, aged four months and three years, in their home. We are told, cheerfully, that even though Richard Williams has worked only since 1962 and will have contributed (as of mid-1975) less than $3,000 to Social Security, that he and his family are protected by more than $526,000 worth of promises from the federal government—a tax-free bonus of more than a half million dollars made up of potential death, disability, survivors', and retirement insurance benefits.

How can a program be labeled bad when it sounds so good? The answer rests in the financial fudging, manipulation, and out-and-out lies used to compute the Richard Williams "typical example."* Rather than reaping a financial windfall, the Richard Williams family and the millions of other American families just like them suffer a secret loss every year. Here's how it works.

Using the Social Security death and survivors' benefits as an example, the administration describes the "value" of Richard Williams's government life insurance as $213,762. They make the following assumptions: If Williams should die in 1975, Mary and the two young children would be entitled to receive $651.60 per month in a family benefit check until Williams's younger child (now four months old) reaches eighteen. As this is currently 212 months off, the family benefit checks would total $138,139. At this point Mary's benefit would stop, but the two children would continue to receive $558.40 per month until the older child (now three years old) reaches age twenty-two, assuming he remains a full-time student. This additional sixteen-month benefit would total $8,934.40. Once the Williams family check is reduced to a single student's benefit (for the younger child) of $279.20 per month, the checks continue for an additional thirty-two months which, according to the administration, adds another $8,934.40 to Williams's "current

---

* It is not the purpose here to impune the motives of either the Research Institute of America or the California Taxpayers' Lobby, as both groups appear to have acted on what was felt to be reliable government information.

protection level." So far the benefits in this example total $156,263.20 including the $255 to cover part of Williams's burial expenses.

But, says the government, this isn't all. Though Mary Williams stops getting her own survivor's benefit when her younger child reaches eighteen, she may apply for widow's benefits as early as sixty and receive a monthly check for $266.20. Assuming Mrs. Williams survives to age seventy-eight, this annuity, says the administration, would be worth $57,499.20.

There you have it, we are told; for a modest tax contribution of less than $3,000, Richard Williams can rest easy with the assurance that his family is protected to the tune of $213,762.20. Further, we are assured, Williams's family protection level will rise each year he lives as long as his wages continue rising with the cost of living.

The trouble is that Williams's "protection" costs more than his government tells him it does and is worth considerably less. In the first place, Richard Williams's Social Security bill has not been $3,000 during his working life, but $6,000. For some unfathomable reason the Social Security Administration persists in telling tax-payers that the cost of the program is the amount in his paycheck box marked "FICA" even though it is now widely understood that the employer is required to double that amount before sending the tax to the government.

In a June 1974 statement published in *The New York Times,* Commissioner Cardwell described the employer's portion of the Social Security tax as "simply a cost of doing business" and thus not part of the employee's cost of protection. This is, as University of Chicago economist Milton Friedman has labeled it, classic bureaucratic double-think. Such a conclusion, on Cardwell's part, cannot be supported.

During 1975 the hypothetical Richard Williams (and anyone else earning $14,100 or more in wages) will have $824.85 deducted from his pay for Social Security. This amount, however, will not satisfy the Internal Revenue Service, which acts as collection agent for the Social Security Administration. The total IRS expects from Williams's employer as a result of Williams's labor is $1,649.70. What is to be gained by extending the sham of telling Williams and others like him that the "cost" of his Social Security protection is $824.85 when the government demands $1,649.70 and will not accept one penny less?

The endless economic wrangle over who really bears the cost of the "other" $824.85 simply clouds the issue. What is being studied here is the number of dollars the federal government demands in order to make the promises made to Richard Williams. The answer is $1,649.70 in 1975 and a total of nearly $12,000 thus far in Williams's career.

Still, one might ask, why quibble over $3,000 when Williams's family is promised thirty-five times that amount should he die during 1975? The extra $3,000 is important because it compounds the incredible fraud of labeling Williams's Social Security promise as being "worth" $213,762.20. It is in fact worth so much less that Williams and others like him are actually overpaying the government more than 100 percent very year!

The real value of Social Security's promise to the Richard Williams family is less than 51 percent of what the government says it is. The real cost of making this promise is less than 35 percent of what the government demands.

To simplify matters we will accumulate the Social Security Administration's overstatements as we go along. When the federal government promises Richard Williams that his family will get $651 per month for 212 months, one assumes that administration actuaries are aware that it does not cost $138,139 to make such a promise. Since the Social Security Administration employs more than fifty full-time actuaries and many others on a part-time or consulting basis, we can be certain they are familiar with the financial truth that it doesn't cost $100 to offer someone $1 a month for 100 months.

Thus, if a man wants to assure that upon his death someone will receive one dollar per month for 100 months, he doesn't need

$100 in insurance, but only $81.64. This amount will cover the promise at even the most conservative interest rates. Furthermore, if the one-dollar-per-month payments aren't to begin until 200 months after the death, only $35.54 in insurance would cover all 100 payments.

The real question the Richard Williamses of America must ask is "How much would have to be deposited in savings to assure one's family of $651 per month for 212 months?" Even if we assume a routine passbook rate of 5 percent, we find the cost of that promise is not $138,139 but $91,261. The government has over-stated their promise to Richard Williams by 34 percent, or $46,878.

To continue, the government then promises that once the youngest Williams child reaches eighteen the family benefit will be reduced to $558.40 a month, but will remain at this level for sixteen more months. By carefully multiplying $558.40 times six-teen, the administration concludes for us that this additional prom-ise is worth $8,934.40. Further, since the youngest Williams child would be entitled to a benefit check until he reached twenty-two (as a full-time student), he could receive $279.20 for an additional thirty-two months. This, we are assured, is worth another $8,934.40 to Richard Williams's peace of mind today. Thus the federal prom-ise to Mr. Williams is puffed by another $17,868.80, but, as before, all is not as it seems.

Again, the question to be answered is "How much money would Richard Williams need today to be able to duplicate the government guarantee to his family?" We've already seen that money paid over a number of months has time to earn interest so that the sum total of the payments is not needed at the start. In the case of a total of $8,934.40 due in sixteen monthly installments of $558.40, a fund of $8,619 held at 5 percent interest would cover the payments. In the same manner, payments of $279.20 each month for thirty-two months could be covered with a cash fund of $8,342 and not $8,934.

So far we know the "additional" $17,868.80 is worth no more

than $16,961, but the federal actuaries know a lot more than that. Remember that the first part of Williams's benefits ($651.60 per month) would be payable immediately on his death, but the "additions" wouldn't be due to start until 212 months later, when the first benefit runs out, and 228 months later, when the second benefit runs out.

We should then change our question to Richard Williams. How much money, we should ask, does Mr. Williams need now to be able to assure payment of $8,619 beginning more than seventeen years from now, and $8,342 beginning nineteen years from now? The answer is that Williams would need to set aside $6,809 to cover both payments—not $17,868.80 as the administration example implied.

This time the government overstatement of the value of the promise made to Richard Williams is a whopping 61 percent, or $11,060, bringing the total discovered "error" thus far to $57,938.

The worst is to come. The Social Security Administration values the widow's annuity due Mary Williams at $57,499.20 because she is entitled to receive $266.20 each month at age sixty and is expected to live another eighteen years afterward. We have seen enough so far to realize the price has been set much too high.

Richard Williams could bequeath his thirty-five-year-old wife a $266.20-per-month pension when she reached sixty by setting aside $9,073 today. Surely one of those administration actuaries knew that $57,499.20 is overstating the government's offer to Mr. Williams by an incredible 534 percent.

Why wasn't Richard Williams told the truth?—that his federal insurance death benefit/burial fee/annuity package had the wrong price tag attached. Instead of $213,762, the real potential value of the offer to Williams is $107,143. It is impossible that an entire bureau of federal actuaries did not realize that the "Williams example," so proudly displayed, is in fact a 99.5 percent error which overstated the real value of the government protection by more than $106,000.

Nor is this all of the "Williams example." * In the full reports designed "to show you in exact dollar terms just how much your Social Security is worth," we are told that families like Mr. Williams's are due potential benefits of "over a half million dollars" on taxes already paid. This figure is so absurdly false that it deserves no more mention than as an example of the depth of the administration's deceit.

The half-million-dollar amount (over $526,000) is arrived at by adding to the already discussed $213,762.00 additional "potential benefits" of $205,394.10 in disability protection and still another $107,172.00 in retirement annuities. The last two "benefits" were calculated in the same manner as the death benefits we've already looked at.

No American worker could discover a more lucid illustration of the intelligence estimate his government has made of him than by studying this example. In order to reach the "potential benefit" of $526,328.30, workers like Richard Williams would have to discover a way to become 100 percent disabled at thirty-five, die at thirty-five, and still work to age sixty-five before dying again at the mathematically average age of seventy-eight. To add up three different benefit programs which could *never* be paid to the same family during the same lifetime must establish some record for lunacy.

These examples are not, of course, administration mistakes. They have been carefully designed to produce the precise attitude which exists today. The American Social Security system is based upon the belief, by people like Richard Williams, that a promise of $213,762.20 (in death and annuity benefits alone) is a fair return for the $1,544 in Social Security taxes the government demanded of Williams and his employer in 1974. It is sustained by the belief that $1,649, a 6.8 percent increase paid in 1975 will buy a 6.8 percent rise in real protection and keep the system solvent. Neither is true.

* In some publications, the same or similarly computed figures appeared with the family name changed to Jones, Brown, etc.

The truth is that American working families will have less protection per tax dollar in 1975 than they had in 1974. The ratio of taxes-to-benefits will become silently worse next year and every year thereafter. What will grow are the taxes paid by wage earners and the promises needed to make the taxes seem just—as on July 1, 1972, when then Social Security Commissioner Robert M. Ball assured Americans that the 20 percent rise in Social Security taxes, set for 1973, would count fully "toward the benefits that will be payable to them and their families in the future." In fact the rise in Social Security taxes during 1973 and 1974 came to more than 46 percent—the largest two-year hike in history—and made the protection picture even bleaker for working Americans than before. The benefit increases only seemed to be going to them.

Polishing Up the Numbers to a Blinding Sparkle

Not unexpectedly, Americans don't like to be taxed. In most surveys the tax we seem to like least is the income tax—so visible on each paycheck and seeming to penalize our ambition. On the other hand, a poll taken in 1974 for the National Broadcasting Company showed that fewer than 20 percent of those responding even mentioned Social Security in answer to a question asking for a list of "the five most disliked taxes." It is astonishing, then, that in 1975 more than half of all American taxpayers will pay *more* in Social Security tax than in income tax. Why do we pay so willingly? The difference is governmental marketing. We believe we are buying security.

To test our beliefs, we should look at the administration's most shining example, again the Williams family. As we have seen, what Richard Williams was promised is at least three times more than he could ever receive in family protection. Rather than waste time attacking the ridiculous $526,000 promise, let's look instead at the so-called "death and survivors' protection" offered American taxpayers like Williams.

In the government's example, thirty-five-year-old Richard Williams died in 1974 leaving behind a thirty-five-year-old wife and two children aged four months and three years who were both to go to college. His Social Security tax bill that year was $1,544, which came entirely from the payroll of the company employing Williams although only half the amount appeared on his paycheck stubs.

The government added up all the benefits it would pay the Williams family in the next forty-three years and declared that Williams's "protection" is worth $213,762.20. We saw later that the actual level of protection is $107,143. But the level of protection is not the same as the cost of protection. The real "cost" is much lower still and the Social Security Administration knows this very well. The fact that most Americans don't know the real price tag for Social Security is what keeps the system afloat.

The problem is that the Social Security Administration expects us to believe whatever they say. If they tell us, as they did in scores of newspaper defenses of the system in 1974 and 1975, that we "should think of Social Security as group insurance," they expect that we take them at their word. Yet when describing our benefits, the administration uses such childishly illogical examples that any comparison to insurance is impossible.

This is what the federal government would rather we didn't understand. If someone like Richard Williams wants to know the real cost of the protection his Social Security taxes buy, he would certainly not add up the amounts on the next forty-three years of benefit checks he's promised. That would be assuming that money has no value and so would earn no interest at all. The government seems to understand very well that money has value when offering its own treasury bonds to private investors. The Federal Reserve regularly offers to pay citizens 8 percent interest or more for accepting its treasury notes.

Thus Richard Williams and others would certainly agree that assigning the nominal value of 5 percent to his federal promise and reducing it to $107,143 is certainly reasonable. But he shouldn't stop there. He should be asking himself about the actual chance that he will die at thirty-five. After all the true cost of offering a promise is based upon the likelihood of having to make good. Insurance, as the administration is fond of calling its program, is the science of assigning value to certain risks. The risk that Richard Williams will die at age thirty-five, as an actuary can confirm, is less than three chances in 1,000.

Now we can take a better look at the system its commissioner, James B. Cardwell, labeled in early 1975 "the greatest and most generous source of protection for the American worker." If we assume a group of 1,000 workers who at age thirty-five paid in 1974 the maximum Social Security tax of $1,544 (there are more than 1.6 million in this category), we arrive at total "contributions" to the government of more than $1.5 million. Since only three of these 1,000 taxpayers were likely to collect the death, survivors', and annuity benefits promised in 1974, the risk taken by the government for the $1.5 million is $321,429 or three times the $107,143 cost we've established. That's less than one fourth of the tax collected, leaving more than $1.2 million.

Obviously the Social Security system is not the most efficient way for people like Richard Williams to solve what is essentially a problem of risk protection. For Mr. Williams to guarantee his family total future payments of $213,762.20, should he die at thirty-five, what he really needs is an estate of slightly more than $107,000 available in the year he dies. This does not cost $1,544 to create.

Any insurance company, using a standard rate table, could sell Richard Williams or any other average thirty-five-year-old all the financial protection needed to duplicate the death, survivors', and annuity benefits in our current example for $544.50 in premiums.

Keep in mind that the $1,544 paid on behalf of Richard Williams in 1974 was used to create *all* of the benefits his family could receive on his behalf after his death that year. This assumes all of the burial benefit, all of family benefit checks for the following eighteen years, all the student benefits for the next four years, as well as all eighteen years of the widow's annuity to Mary Williams. Yet Richard Williams could have bought the $107,143 in life insurance necessary to pay those bills for $544.50.* The system which promised to be "the best financial security for young families" overcharged Richard Williams $1,000 in the year he died.

Stop!

This is where most Americans usually quit reading. After all, insurance is a bore—something to be discussed only after we've run out of excuses for avoiding the insurance man and his briefcase full of options and clauses. This is also how a modest 1 percent payroll tax called Social Security, enacted in 1935, grew to become a $75 billion colossus accounting for one third of all our tax dollars. We have refused to look at what it has become: an insatiable taxing device masquerading as an insurance system. Social Security could not have become what it has without having chosen the perfect disguise; one we don't like to look at.

As an author, I ask your indulgence. I have no connection whatever with the insurance industry, nor is it necessary that we understand all of insurance to see what is happening to us. What is important for most working Americans to understand is that when they pay 300 percent to 400 percent too much for "security," their lives are not secure.

Rather than studying the intricacies of insurance, what we need to know is how what is promised, and what is not promised, can alter lives. For instance, the most important difference between the $1,544 protection the federal government demanded that Richard Williams buy, in the hypothetical year he died, and the $544.50 protection he could have bought himself, was *not* the $1,000 in

---

* The amount is calculated on the basis of $107,143 in five-year renewable term insurance, purchased at age thirty-five, including waiver of premium for disability, at a rate of $5.082 per 1,000.

cash the family lost. What Mary Williams and her two children lost when Richard died while "covered" by Social Security was the right to direct their own financial future.

What we must understand is that while the Social Security benefits available to the Williams family are worth $107,143 in the year Mr. Williams dies and the benefits of the private insurance are worth the same, Mary Williams's rights to use the Social Security money on her family's behalf are severely limited by Social Security regulations.

Had Richard Williams died with $544.50 in term life insurance, Mary would have received immediately $107,143 in cash with the right to seek the financial counseling she might need to manage her and her children's future. As insurance proceeds, the money would be fully tax-free.

Under Social Security, Mary Williams has few decisions to make and those she has do her little good. In the first place, Mrs. Williams has no legal rights to the cash value of her Social Security benefits. Regardless of her financial condition at the time her husband died, Mrs. Williams must accept the monthly payment schedule determined by Social Security regulations. This payment schedule has nothing to do with the Williams family's present situation, or Mary Williams's plans for the future; only Richard Williams's past earnings are a factor. The so-called $213,762.20 in benefits the Social Security system promised Richard Williams's family will take forty-three years to reach them no matter what is best for Mary and the children.

The difference between having $107,143 and having an equal value promised in the future is astonishing, as we shall see.

Social Security promises the Williams family a monthly benefit of $651.60 during the years the children are young. Let's assume that instead of Social Security, Richard Williams could have chosen to insure himself for the same $107,143, which would now be available to Mary. We will also assume that, like many young widows with children to support, Mary Williams decides she will invest her insurance money only where she can get perfect safety.

She will find many large, conservatively managed, savings institutions ready to offer her a return of 7.5 percent on her $107,143 deposit. She will also find that her monthly interest payments come to $670. The fact is that if Mary Williams had her own $107,143 to manage, she could pay herself 3 percent *more* than Social Security offers every month and never touch the original $107,143!

Keep in mind that under Social Security the Williams family benefit would be lowered, when the younger child reaches eighteen, to $558.40 per month. Yet as long as Mary Williams chose to leave her insurance money on deposit at the same rate, the $670 per month she might have had would remain constant. At this point Mrs. Williams's private benefits would be outpaying Social Security by 20 percent each month and still she would not have depleted the original $107,143.

When, sixteen months later, the Williams family's Social Security benefit dropped again (because the older Williams child reached twenty-two) to $279.20 per month, the private interest fund need not have stopped. Only now $670 a month would allow Mary Williams to offer her family 140 percent more than she could under Social Security. At the risk of sounding redundant, it should be added that the $107,143 would still be intact.

Under Social Security "protection," the worst years for Mary Williams would come next.

Once the younger Williams child turns twenty-two (assuming he or she has been attending college full-time), the government no longer considers Mary Williams a "mother" and so her mother's benefits, as well as any children's benefits, cease. In the eyes of the Social Security Administration Mrs. Williams has become a "widow" and, under the regulations, the widow of a deceased worker cannot claim any benefits before she reaches sixty. An exception could be made for Mrs. Williams were she found to be totally disabled to the extent she was physically incapable of earning more than $32 a week. Short of this, however, Mary Williams would find herself at fifty-seven facing three years without any benefits. Once again, the private bank account that might have been could have paid another

$26,800 during this period without ever falling below the face amount of Richard Williams's insurance.

To this point, the $1,544 "family protection" Richard Williams and his employer paid for in the year he died has paid the Williams family a total of $156,007 with $57,499 left to be paid Mary Williams as a widow's annuity. The $544.50 private plan Williams might have purchased could have been used to pay $201,000 by the time Mary Williams reached sixty and still have left her with the original $107,143 to use for her retirement or any other way she saw fit. Once again, the difference between what she could buy for her old age and what the government chooses to dole out is substantial.

At age sixty, Richard Williams's widow is told by the Social Security Administration that she has the following choice regarding her old-age benefits: She may wait for her benefits to begin at age sixty-five, at which time she would be eligible for a monthly benefit of $372.30. Or she may take her benefits earlier and receive less. If Mrs. Williams chooses to take her benefits immediately, she will begin receiving $266.20—a reduction of 28.5 percent from the monthly check she could have gotten had she waited.

But, under Social Security, Mary Williams has already waited. She has been without any benefits for three years, and so like many others she chooses to begin her widow's annuity immediately—at $266.20 per month. It was probably explained to Mrs. Williams at one of the Social Security Administration local offices that her choice was really not as important as it sounded. If she assumes, for instance, that she will live to the statistically average age for U.S. women of seventy-eight, her reduced benefits will have paid her $57,499.20 by the time she dies, but if she waits for the maximum payment at age sixty-five and still dies at seventy-eight the benefits would be $58,078.80—a difference of less than $580 and hardly worth waiting five years for.

Of course if Mary Williams lives longer than seventy-eight, her decision to take early benefits will have been more and more expensive. In fact, for every month Mrs. Williams lives past age seventy-seven her decision will have cost her another $106.10, so she is better off not thinking about it.

Now let's bring Mrs. Williams back to age sixty and take a look at the kinds of decisions she would have to make under private protection. Her original $107,143 is still intact and probably still capable of paying $670 per month in interest—more than she would ever have received from Social Security. She has a number of choices including these two. She can buy an annuity immediately at age sixty which will guarantee her $761 per month for the rest of her life, or she may wait five years (keeping the $107,143 and the $670-a-month interest income) and buy the annuity then. At age sixty-five, Mrs. Williams's $107,143 would buy her a guarantee of $846 per month—$474 *more* each month than Social Security's "maximum."

Notice that under Social Security Mrs. Williams would receive 28.5 percent less than the age-sixty-five maximum for taking benefits at sixty, but that with a private annuity the difference between the age-sixty benefit ($761) and the age-sixty-five ($846) is less than 10 percent. She chooses to wait until sixty-five.

In the year Richard Williams died it probably never occurred to him that the way in which his tax money was used could make such a vast difference in what he was to leave behind—in fact how secure or insecure he was during any year he lived and worked.

A final summing up of the total Social Security maximum benefits, costing $1,544, and the private plan, costing $1,000 less, looks like this. Assuming Mary Williams and her two children made all the decisions her government expected and lived as long as is actuarially normal, a total of $213,762.20 would have been paid in Social Security benefits. If, however, she had been protected under the private plan (and made the decisions previously mentioned including a pension at sixty-five), she and the children could have received $373,176. How could Richard Williams have known that what was taken from his pay the year he died could make a difference of $159,414 to his wife and children? And keep in mind that

Mary Williams used her private benefits in the most conservative possible way—an insured savings account and an annuity plan.

It is sure to be pointed out that Social Security benefits are not subject to income taxes while private interest and annuity income are subject to such taxes. As a widow with two children who later retires on annuity income, Mary Williams would be liable for $21,788 in total income tax during her life—still leaving her more than $137,000 better off than "tax-free" Social Security. Further, any trust adviser could have told Mrs. Williams how she might have sheltered even more of her husband's insurance benefits from income tax than with the rather simple methods used in our example. We'll take another look at Social Security and the U.S. income tax system later.

It Pays to Live the Way Your Government Expects

Believe it or not, the example of the Richard Williams family under Social Security was the best it could have been for them. As far below private protection levels as Richard Williams left his family, the amounts in the examples we've seen were "maximum" benefits—where we always assumed that Mary and the two children lived as the Social Security Administration regulations demand they do. If they hadn't lived that way, they couldn't have qualified for the "maximum" benefits they got no matter how much Richard Williams and his employer paid in taxes.

Perhaps the single most incredible element of Social Security is the administration's insistence that the program is insurance while, at the same time, basing the entire benefits structure on a handbook of regulations the use of which would land most insurance-company officials in jail. The regulations governing the payment of Social Security benefits to the worker who paid taxes (or his beneficiaries) contain more than 500 circumstances under which the government will not pay.

Under the "unstated exclusions" doctrine of the Federal Trade Commission and the majority of state insurance codes, a private insurance plan which cost as much as Social Security and contained as many grounds for not paying benefits, or reducing the advertised maximum, would not be allowed to stay in business.

The case of the Richard Williams family is typical of the circumstances in which most middle-income Americans would find themselves when confronting the maze of Social Security regulations. In real life it is quite unlikely that Mary Williams and her two children would actually receive all the maximum benefits Mr. Williams thought they would.

To understand the real financial tragedy thirty-five-year-old Mary Williams faced when Richard died, we should set the scene a little more fully. Since Mr. Williams paid the maximum Social Security tax we can assume he was earning at the yearly rate of at least $13,200 in the year (1974) he died. If he faced the usual assortment of payroll taxes, Richard Williams probably took home $770 per month. With both a three-year-old and a four-month-old at home, it's unlikely Mary Williams was working when Richard died.

Once the shock of her husband's death has been realized and a few details have been put in order by well-meaning friends, Mary Williams must put together a plan for supporting her family. Karen, the four-month-old, and the three-year-old Donald now rely on Mrs. Williams who hasn't worked in four years and then made less than half the amount Richard was taking home when he died.

About a week after Richard's death, Mrs. Williams finds herself in a neighborhood office of the Social Security Administration. She is told that based on Richard's earnings record, the family is entitled to a monthly benefit of $651.60 as long as at least one of the children is under eighteen and living at home. One thing, though, she is told: in order to receive these maximum benefits as a "mother," she must not earn more than $2,400 per year. Like most women in her circumstances, Mary Williams is glad to get the news that she will have a regular income. She does not fully think about what has happened to her.

Mary listens appreciatively while the Social Security clerk explains that her family's benefits were figured based on Richard Williams's "average taxable earnings" during the years he worked. It is made to seem quite fair that a kind of average be taken of the years during which Mr. Williams paid high Social Security taxes and the years he paid lower taxes. This kind of "fairness" is what keeps Social Security afloat. Consider the same kind of thinking in another area and then see how fair it seems to you.

Let's assume you have been working for five years and getting regular raises each year. You have also been seeing an insurance agent and buying all the life insurance you could afford each year as a protection for your family. The first year you bought a $5,000 policy, the second year an increase to a $10,000 policy, and so on, increasing your premiums each year to pay for $5,000 more in protection than the year before. Now, in the fifth year of your plan, paying much more than in your first, you are covered by $25,000 in life insurance. We must also assume, sadly, that you die while paying premiums on your $25,000 policy.

Now your grief-stricken wife goes to see your insurance agent with the $25,000 policy in one hand and your death certificate in the other, expecting to walk out with a check for $25,000. Sorry, she is told, but the company figures benefits on "average premiums paid" not on the face amount on the policy in the year the policy-holder dies. After all, the agent tells your wife, fair is fair. So your momentarily confused wife watches while the agent makes out a check for $15,000 which represents the "average" value of the premiums you paid during the last five years. It is also the amount of insurance you had three years ago.

Fortunately, the insurance industry, whether by its own scruples or state regulation, does not operate this way. Your premium is paying for a certain risk, on the part of the insurance company, computed for the year in which the premium is being paid. In our last example, a man who dies while paying premiums on a $25,000 policy will leave his beneficiary $25,000. We would accept no less from the insurance industry and we're right.

The fact is that the widely distributed "Social Security maximum benefit," published each year from Baltimore, is little more than an accounting figure—virtually impossible to attain in the year it's released to the public. The reason, of course, is that Social Security taxes go up every year, so that the vast majority of those who die or become disabled or retire in a given year will also have paid taxes during previous, lower, tax years. By the "averaging rule," they or their beneficiaries will receive less than the maximum benefit even though they paid maximum "contributions" in the year of the event in question. While an accumulation of payment makes some sense in the case of retirement benefits, death and disability are simple financial risks. Why, then, do we accept this kind of "fairness" from the federal government?

No matter what else is said about the Social Security Administration's averaging rule, one fact is so hideously wrong—so poisonous—in its contempt for basic justice that it alone should bring the system down. The fact is this: In any given year, a worker who had paid *more* in maximum Social Security taxes will be eligible for a *lower* benefit than a worker who has paid *less* in maximum taxes. You may need to read this over a few times for the real lunacy to become distinct.

Once again, the Social Security Administration has discovered a device for making the bad seem good. In a number of administration booklets published in 1974, the averaging of covered earnings is made to appear an innocent device for attaining fairness in such contexts as "someone at a Social Security office will be glad to help figure your average earnings to see you get the correct benefit." What is not explained in the comforting prose is that the averaging rule nearly always works against the taxpayer.

As long as we have already become familiar with Richard Williams's case history, let's continue with one of Williams's coworkers, John Lewis. Mr. Lewis is remarkably like Mr. Williams except that he is forty-five years old—exactly ten years older than Richard Williams. Both men are married and both have two children. Mr. Lewis's children are also ten years older than Mr. Williams's.

As for Social Security, both Richard Williams and John Lewis have paid the maximum tax all their working lives. Since John Lewis has worked ten years longer than Williams, he has paid 43 percent more in employee/employer taxes—$9,036 where Williams had paid $6,330.

To continue the curious parallel of these two men, we must assume that John Lewis dies on the same day in 1974 as Richard Williams. His wife too (we'll call her Joan) must see about Social Security benefits to support her children.

Joan Lewis is told that the maximum monthly benefit her family has coming is $557.50—not the $651.60 Mary Williams will get. Further, when Joan is first eligible to retire (fifteen years hence, as we assume that she is forty-five), she will qualify for $218 per month instead of the $266 Mary Williams can collect.

Not only does the Lewis family receive lower monthly benefits, they will be eligible for a shorter time. Remember, maximum family benefits are paid only as long as a mother cares for children in school and the Lewis children are ten years older than the Williams children—Mark is ten years old and Lisa is thirteen—so checks will come 120 fewer months.

What "earnings averaging" and the other Social Security rules mean to John Lewis is that for his $1,544 tax level in 1974 he bought a government promise which will add up to $113,013.20 when paid. And that Richard Williams, who paid the *same* 1974 tax, paid $2,706 *less* tax during his working career, and died on the same day, will leave his family $213,762.20—over $100,000 more than Lewis.

What has happened to John Lewis's family represents no level of equity at all. As we have seen before, the real cost of providing Richard Williams $213,762.20 in family benefits is $107,143. Using the same reasoning, the promise being made to John Lewis is worth $66,395, or 38 percent less. We saw that Mr. Williams could duplicate his government protection for $544.50 in private insurance. John Lewis, even though he would pay higher rates for insurance at forty-five, could duplicate his federal promise for $679.75 on his own. Both were paying $1,544 in the year they died.

The average rule was rigged against the Lewis family, and millions of other American families, from the start. In this case the administration told us what they were doing and apparently no one noticed what the practice really meant. The federal pamphlet *Your Social Security Earnings Record* says in clear language: "Benefits under the retirement, survivors, and disability insurance program are figured from your earnings covered by law, not from the contributions paid." Without even pausing to reflect on how the government can call something "insurance" and then admit in the same sentence that benefits are not related to money actually paid, we must understand what is being done to us.

Simply stated, the averaging rule works this way. The system works by finding an average of your "covered earnings" during your working career. "Covered earnings" are those which fall at or below the maximum Social Security wage base for a given year. In 1975, for instance, the maximum wage base is $14,100, which means a worker earning $10,000 in 1975 would record $10,000 as his "covered earnings," but a worker making $15,000 would record $14,100 since that is the maximum for the year involved. Once you have a list of "covered earnings," you are allowed to drop out your five lowest years. Any covered earnings for the year of death, disablement, or retirement are also ignored. An average of what's left is used to figure the worker's benefit.

Between 1950 and 1975 the Social Security tax level has been raised, officially, eighteen times. Since the maximum payroll tax has traditionally been set at the middle-class earnings level, there are millions of workers who, just like John Lewis, have always paid maximum taxes. Thus, when it comes time to figure benefits, the longer one has worked the further back in time the government reaches to arrive at his "average taxable earnings." The net effect is twofold. The longer you have paid into Social Security the more money you will have been taxed, but for every year in the past the government uses to figure your benefit, the lower that benefit will be because more and more low tax years are averaged in.

The effect of the averaging rule is easy to see. If you have worked the last fifteen years at maximum Social Security levels and your co-worker has worked the last ten, two things will have happened. You will have paid more Social Security tax and he will be eligible for a higher benefit than you. Mrs. Lewis is about to learn the absurd cruelty of this rule.

Before the two widows die, Mary Williams and her family will have received over $100,000 more than Joan Lewis and her family. The government freely admits this difference has nothing to do with family need. The only sin John Lewis committed was working ten years more than Richard Williams, which had the unfortunate statistical effect of lowering Lewis's average. Even if Joan Lewis makes up the age difference by living to be ten years older than Mary Williams (so that Joan, at eighty-eight, would die on the same day as Mary, at seventy-eight) she would still have received $80,000 less in benefits.

We can now return to the day in 1974 that Mary Williams's benefits were first described to her. Having heard about Joan Lewis's experience, Mary was even more appreciative of the $651.60 her family would be receiving. After all, she now knew, things could be worse. But more than the averaging process for computing benefits had been described to Mary. She was also told of the "earnings limitation" under which the family would not get all of its $651.60 if she earned more than $2,400 in any year. "These benefits," the clerk had said, "are designed to replace lost earnings, so, of course they won't be paid in full if you still have earnings."

Again, illogic silently takes the helm. The Richard Williams family *has* lost earnings; they lost them the moment Mr. Williams died. It was Richard's earnings that Mary Williams lost and it was his earnings that he had been told he was protecting with his Social Security tax. Now the government informs Mary that they consider her earnings, if she chooses to work, to have partially replaced her husband's and thus they will reduce her benefit. This is obscene. If the Williams family will get less Social Security because Mary Williams works, then at least in part, it is her work and not Richard's federal insurance that will pay the bills. To the extent which Mary's earnings pay the bills, it is she who is acting as the family's insurance, not Social Security. Why should Richard have been forced to pay taxes for that?

The Social Security earnings limitation, like the averaging rule, inflicts widespread damage. Unlike the averaging rule, however, the damage will be felt by the entire nation. For when Mary Williams understands how the income limitation operates, she will probably not work and so the income tax her husband was paying will not even be partially replaced. The tax load will simply fall on others.

For the Williams family, things will work this way: As long as Mary Williams is not earning outside income and is caring for her two children at home, the Social Security Administration will send a family benefit of $651.60 each month. If, however, Mrs. Williams does earn money and in fact earns more than $2,400 in a year or $200 in a month, the family will lose $1 for every $2 she earns as a deduction from the Social Security benefit. In the case of the Williams family, as much as $93.20 per month could be lost this way. The earnings limitation may be America's most perverse tax.

Let's assume that Mary can find a way to arrange babysitters and other help so that she can work afternoons at a local dress shop. The manager knows the family and has offered Mary thirty hours per week at $3.00 an hour. Mary feels she can use the extra $90 a week. The after-tax amount would, with Social Security, bring the family closer to what Richard was taking home. After the initial rush of help from neighbors following Richard's death, Mary now finds she needs to call in outside workmen more and more often to make repairs her husband used to make. She takes the job and, as the law demands, reports her earnings to the Social Security Administration.

It is a full year of babysitters, quick lunches, friends' favors, and the like before Mrs. Williams realizes the real consequences of her decision to take a job. She gets a letter from the Social Security Administration notifying her that because she earned $4,680 the previous year, during the coming year the amount over the "earnings limitation" will be deducted from her benefit. Thus the Williams's $651.60 monthly benefit will shrink to $558.40 per month for one year. If Mary keeps the job, she is told, a similar reduction will be made next year. It's time to figure out how much the federal government is really taxing her income, Mrs. Williams decides.

Since the Williams benefit check will be reduced $93.20 each month for a year, a total of $1,118.40 in annual income will be lost to the family. This is equal to $21.51 each week. Thus Mary's $90-per-week job is really adding to her family's income by only $68.49 a week when she subtracts what Social Security deducts from the family benefit. Her $3.00-an-hour job really nets Mrs. Williams $2.28, from which federal income tax, state income tax, and (lest we forget) her own Social Security payroll tax must be deducted.* Adding in the babysitting costs and the clothes she needs to keep her job, Mary Williams sees that her time away from her children has done very little good. She thanks the clothing-store manager and quits.

When labor which would bring a worker $90 instead brings $68.49, the government policy involved is an income tax. If we add in all the other taxes on Mary Williams's paycheck, we get total weekly deductions of $30.59 which makes for an interesting comparison when she looks at a co-worker's paystub. Another worker at the clothing store, making the same money and claiming the same three exemptions, takes home $80.92 of her $90 pay—a

---

* Like many U.S. taxpayers, Mary Williams pays *more* Social Security payroll tax than income tax.

total 10.1 percent tax rate. The net result of Mary Williams's same thirty hours work is $59.41—a 34 percent tax rate, or the same as someone earning nearly four times what Mary does. The difference between the protection Richard Williams could have bought with his $1,544 tax, and what he was forced to buy, continues to grow.

Thanks to the continuing and sadistic maze of Social Security regulations, Mrs. Williams has left more than her job when she left the clothing store. She left the only chance she had to increase her retirement benefit on her own. Had she remained at work, at thirty-five, Mary could have accumulated enough Social Security credits, during high taxation future years, to insure herself a larger pension than the $266.20 she is already promised. Instead, for the next eighteen years, Mary is actively discouraged from working by an "earnings limitation" which won't be lifted until she is fifty-three. Since her own retirement credits would take at least ten years to accumulate,* Mary will probably never have her own pension. What she will have is eighteen years under an earnings limitation which is, in fact, an income tax four times greater than it should be.

There's More

For American workers who die or become disabled with only one child or without children, the earnings limitation is even more destructive. Had Richard Williams died leaving a single child instead of two, he would have left his family a benefit of $558.40 instead of $651.60 on the somewhat arbitrary assumption that a family with one child needs 14 percent less than a family with two children. Because of the internal workings of the earnings limitation, a mother caring for one child can lose up to half the

---

* According to law, an American worker born after 1929 needs ten years of work under Social Security to qualify for any retirement benefit on his own.

family benefit for earning more than the government allows. If Mary Williams had one child at the time of her husband's death, a job paying $115 per week would drop the family benefit check from $558.40 to $408.40—a loss of 27 percent. If Richard and Mary had been childless when he died, the same $115-per-week job would have reduced her $279.20 monthly check to $129.20—costing her 54 percent of the insurance protection Richard thought his taxes were buying.

Can we really have sat by while our government fashioned a compulsory insurance system so obtuse and unreasoning that five thirty-five-year-old men, who all pay $1,650 in 1975 Social Security tax, are "insured" for vastly different amounts—just because one has three children, one has two children, one has a single child, one is childless, and the last one is single? If the government is so certain that the number of children is the only measure of insurance need, why not allow those who are protected least a chance to pay the least?

Where the Social Security Administration and the U.S. Congress are creative is in the designing of regulations which limit benefits. We have been sold a compulsory public insurance system because, in the words of former HEW Secretary Wilbur Cohen, "no private insurance company could do as well." What he might have said was that none would be allowed to perform as poorly with so many aspects of fraud.

When Mary Williams left the Social Security office she knew of only two regulations which limit benefit payments: the earnings averaging rule which cost Joan Lewis so dearly, and the earnings limitation which would eventually cost Mary her job. While these two rules are certainly the major causes of benefit limitations, Social Security regulations contain plenty of others. Here are a few that stand out:

1. Mary may not remarry. Although Mary Williams is in the prime of her life at thirty-five and may wish to remarry, federal regulations say that if she does remarry she is no longer entitled to

benefits under Richard's insurance. She may, of course, qualify for benefits under her new husband's Social Security, but the question still remains one of determining what Richard Williams really bought in the way of protection for his wife. Did he realize that the $1,544-a-year level of protection he thought he was leaving his wife and family actually bought Mary Williams a series of can't-win decisions? She can't go to work without being taxed at a rate many times higher than her co-workers. If she remarries, $20,000 of the money Richard thought he was leaving will not be paid.

Since Mary's new husband (likely to be near Richard's age) will probably be taxed enough in the future to qualify for a larger retirement benefit than Richard's was to have been, Richard's will not be paid to Mary. Deduct another $57,499 from Mr. Williams's federal promise—reduced by 36 percent if his young wife chooses not to remain a widow.

2. Mary must qualify as a good mother in the eyes of the government. According to paragraph 313 of the Social Security *Handbook,* Mary would not get her benefits if the government determined her children were not "in her care." Thus if Mary and her mother were to decide that either one of the two children were better off living with their grandparents, a federal determination could be made that Mary no longer "measurably controls the child's upbringing," and thereby fails to qualify for mother's benefits.

3. The two Williams children must continue their schooling after high school or their benefits stop. Based on this rule, the government obligation to the Williams family would drop by $20,000, which would be paid to no one.

4. The Social Security Administration is not promising that Richard Williams's benefits *will* be paid, only that they *can* be paid if the laws stay the same in the future and Mary and the kids agree to live the way the government expects. Whether the $213,762.45 promise is worth only $107,143 is less important than the fact that the money is not Mrs. Williams's to control.

As an example, Mary Williams could have used her private

$107,143 fund to pay her family $670-per-month interest. She could have added her $90-per-week earnings at no penalty. She also would have had the option to decline monthly interest checks on the $107,143 and let the money accumulate. Let's say she decided to live on interest payments for two years while she completed training as a medical technician. She could then allow interest payments to stop while the family lived on her salary and their $107,143 grew. At the end of five years the money would have grown to $153,818—enough to provide $961 in monthly interest payments or to add to the children's college fund or Mary's retirement income.

By contrast the money lost by failing to meet Social Security regulations is never repaid. Benefits deducted for earnings-limitation "violations" are lost. If the children don't go to college, the $20,000 in over-eighteen payments are gone. Should Mary have died before reaching sixty with a private fund of money paying her interest, the interest or all the money would pass to whomever she had designated in her will—well over a $100,000 estate years after her husband died. Under Social Security, Mary Williams's death at fifty-eight would mean a signal to a computer in Baltimore telling it not to pay $57,499.20, which would have been her pension. The money would go nowhere.

5. Those who can afford to "insure" their Social Security benefits have a much better chance of getting them. Social Security regulations say that not all "income" is income—only what one earns by working is subject to earnings-limitation penalties. Rental income, interest from stocks and bonds, prizes, tax-free trust fund payments, and private insurance benefits are ignored. What this means is that a family that can afford both the Social Security tax and the private insurance we've mentioned can have both benefits. Richard Williams and his employer paid $128.60 each month for his Social Security coverage in the year Mr. Williams died. The private plan would have cost $45.37 a month and more than doubled the family's protection, but the Williams's budget wouldn't allow the extra cost.

If Mary had both the interest income from private insurance and a Social Security benefit, she would have been allowed by the government to keep both—a total income of $1,321 a month. She would not have needed to leave her children for an outside job or consider remarrying for economic reasons or take her smaller Social Security pension early. But Richard didn't have the extra protection because he couldn't afford it, and besides he hadn't heard that Social Security needs to be insured by more money to be certain one can collect what he's already paid for. There's a lot he probably didn't know.

Did Richard Williams realize he was leaving federal bureaucrats that kind of power over his wife's ideas concerning her own children's well-being? Whatever pretenses the government makes about its "group insurance" program, Social Security, it must always be kept in mind that when social agencies handle our money they always impose some notion of "contemporary morality" over how that money will be distributed. No matter how often we are told the program is insurance under which "higher taxes pay for higher benefits," the money is still dispensed as though it were charity from the federal coffers. Thus, a widow is seen to need charity, but a woman who remarries does not; a mother in the home needs charity, but a mother who works does not; a mother who cares for her children in her home needs charity, but a woman who allows her children to be out of her "parental control" does not.

Millions of Americans, in the same position as Richard Williams, forget that for the amounts they pay in federal Social Security "contributions," their beneficiaries need not live under the rules of social agency charity. Would you buy a private insurance policy with these kinds of limitations? Would you allow a bank officer to ask questions about how you live before he let you withdraw your money? Most of us seem to know the answers to these questions and yet we continue to let the government handle our insurance money as though it were theirs.

What If Richard Williams Had Lived?

There will always be those who simply must believe—whose deeply rooted faith that the governmental bureaucracy must be on their side far outweighs any fear of being cheated. These people will tell themselves, "Richard Williams just died too soon—before all the automatic benefit raises, that came with our tax rise, could take effect."

After all, they will point out, didn't Richard Williams die in 1974, so that only his covered earnings up through 1973 could be used to determine his benefit? And, after all, wasn't 1973 only the first year of the really big tax increases for Social Security? So how could the new benefit formula have a chance to work in his case? Give the system a chance, they will urge. And they will join the generation of victims.

It is true that the "monster tax" years for Social Security didn't really begin until 1973. In all the previous years of payroll deduction, with the exception of 1956, the tax never rose more than $65 in a year. Then came the tidal wave. In 1973 the employee/employer tax swelled $328 from the year before—five times more than the average tax rise in the past and by far the largest increase in the system's history.

But on July 1, 1972, the Social Security Administration told us what was going to happen and assured the American taxpayer, officially, he needn't worry. While the tax base would rise 20 percent, said Social Security Commissioner Robert M. Ball, "every one of the 28.1 million men, women and children on the benefit rolls will receive the increase automatically."

Further, the administration soothed, the 1974 rise in the tax base would not be as steep (11 percent as compared with 20 percent in 1973), and "those additional earnings counted toward the benefits that would be payable to [today's taxpayers] and their families in the future."

It all sounded fair—a 20 percent tax rise for a 20 percent rise in benefits—and besides, the new taxes were to be applied to higher benefits in the future, just the way insurance is supposed to work. Once again, as before, they were playing with the numbers and we didn't notice.

In the first place, the 1973 Social Security tax went up more than 20 percent—more than the benefit increases—but that wasn't in the administration's press release. At the same time that the wage-base maximum went from $9,000 to $10,800, which is 20 percent, the tax rate went from 5.2 percent to 5.85 percent—adding another $140.40 to the maximum tax and making the true tax increase 35 percent.

While it was true that the average retirement check to America's nearly 15 million over sixty-five in 1973 did rise 20 percent, from $148 per month to $177, the extra $29 per month didn't come from any newly generous tax/insurance system. It came from the more than 30 million working Americans (out of the 90 million that Social Security covers) who allowed themselves to be taxed another $27 per month to pay the bill.

But it is a good guess that it wasn't the few extra dollars in 1973 retirement checks that lulled American workers into accepting a 35 percent tax increase. It was more likely the promise that their taxes were buying them more protection—the assurance that they would get their money's worth with immediate new benefits payable to them or their families. Richard Williams probably shared that confidence.

Richard Williams, we will recall, was alive in 1972 when the Social Security Administration made its announcement about his future. He lived through 1973 and paid the 35 percent extra like millions of others. He even lived a while during 1974 and saw his tax rise another 22 percent,* but none of that amount counted toward his death, survivors', and annuity benefits because Social

---

* The new 1974 maximum wage base was $13,200 instead of the $12,000 the administration predicted.

Security rules stipulate the "average covered earnings" be calculated up to the year *before* death. So only the 35 percent, 1973, tax rise affected Mr. Williams's family benefit. And the government press release was correct when it said Mr. Williams's higher taxes would mean higher benefits than were paid before the tax increase. Here comes some more number magic from your federal government.

What the administration press release didn't say was how much of the 35 percent tax increase would actually go toward increasing the protection of American workers. But nobody asked. Had Richard Williams died in 1973 instead of 1974 the family benefit he left behind would not include any of the new "tax increase" money, because the calculations used to determine the benefit would have stopped with 1972—before the tax rise. It would not, then, have been as high as the $651.60 the family got a year later. It would have been $631.30 and it would have surprised a lot of people.

The 35 percent in additional Social Security tax that Richard Williams paid during the year before his death affected his own family benefits by less than 4 percent! If he had lived a year longer than he did, and seen his Social Security tax increase another 22 percent, his family benefits would have increased by only 3.5 percent.

Would we have paid so quietly if we had known?

For Mr. Williams and many others like him, it worked out this way. Dying in 1974 meant a government commitment in funds to his family of $213,762.20 over the next forty-three years. Dying in 1975, with his children a year older, would have meant a government commitment of $213,001.30 to his family. The almost incomprehensible truth is that having paid a 22 percent tax increase the year before, Richard Williams was actually owed $700 *less* than he was before the increase.

There is nothing unusual about the Williams family or their benefits. Any typical American family would have been victimized the same way by Social Security increases. But perhaps family-benefit examples, where children get older more quickly than Social Security gets bigger, are difficult to follow.

All Social Security benefits, whether paid for death, disability, or retirement, are based on a single number which the administration calls the "primary insurance amount," or PIA. When a single worker retires his Social Security pension is the amount of his PIA. If he is married and his wife is also retirement age, the total benefit will be his PIA plus 50 percent more. In the same way, Richard Williams's family benefit was figured by beginning with the PIA amount based on his average earnings. Rather than understanding how a PIA is figured, all we have to know is that all Social Security benefits begin with this number and that no current worker can be eligible for higher benefits unless his PIA is increased to begin with by paying more tax. It's a good simple number to keep your eye on to see where Social Security is taking you.

In 1972, the last year before the colossal Social Security tax increases, a thirty-three-year-old American worker paying the maximum payroll tax would have had a PIA of $350.70. Again, this means if he became totally disabled in that year he would be eligible for $350.70 a month in benefits. If he died in 1972 the most his family could receive would have been $616.70—a number the administration computed by beginning with $350.70, etc.

Every year since then our typical wage earner pays the maximum Social Security tax, which in turn raises his PIA. He pays 35 percent more in 1973, 22 percent more in 1974, and 7 percent more in 1975. In three years his Social Security taxes have risen a total of 76 percent above 1972 levels—a total of $714 per year in new taxes, or more tax increase than the previous twenty-five years *combined*. In 1976, including all his new taxes, the worker's PIA is $396.90, which is only 13 percent higher than 1972. The maximum the worker can leave his family, based on the higher PIA, is $694.60—only 12.6 percent more than in 1972. He has seen his additional taxes for Social Security "count toward higher benefits," just as the administration told him. What they didn't tell him was that the taxes would grow five times faster than his new benefits.

There is no escaping the conclusion that the new Social Security taxes of the mid-seventies weren't intended to improve the system; only to stave off disaster. All of the more than $16 billion in new payroll tax since 1972 has gone to finance new benefits for a nonworking population now growing faster than the American workforce. There was no money left to improve things for those still on the job, so instead of a meaningful raise in insurance protection we got press releases.

What is true is that millions of American families are currently forced to pay for a system which was bankrupt before their working careers began. What we didn't realize is that bankruptcy in a government program doesn't look or act the same as bankruptcy elsewhere. The Social Security checks have not stopped; they simply come more and more from general revenue instead of trust funds. The administration promises have not stopped; they are now backed with projections instead of cash. And finally, the government's Social Security advertising has not stopped. It has been, by all measures, the most successful marketing scheme in financial history, continuing to invent methods of making less sound like more and our money seem like their money, while hoping we won't notice.

8] The Generation of Victims

The Social Security system is looking to an entire generation of young Americans for a very large job it has in mind: saving itself. The current generation of Americans under forty has been chosen for the job and they may start immediately, providing they have the following qualifications:

- a willingness to pay from twenty to fifty times as much in Social Security payroll taxes as the generation before them;
- an acceptance of the fact that, but for a small minority, there is no chance they will receive a fair value for their money;
- a sense of personal sacrifice, among the women in this group, to be subjugated and exploited much worse than the others;
- a desire to underwrite personally the bleak future of this system by allowing the Internal Revenue Service to tax their pay *twice* for the same Social Security "contribution."

In short, the federal administration is looking for a lot of tax-payers who possess that brand of vacant adaptability bureaucrats frequently mislabel "patriotism"—when they issue an impassioned request for those with the deepest wounds to please refrain from hollering.

It is one of the remarkable ironies of today's Social Security that much of the possible opposition from working Americans fails to develop because quotes of future costs are simply unbelievable. Figures of $100,000 or $200,000 in taxes mean very little to today's young worker earning $10,000 to $15,000 a year. ("That can't mean me, can it?") Your government has a surprise in store for you. While Social Security tax is scheduled to become truly incredible in the future, today's young are expected to pay, and will face criminal prosecution if they don't.

If you are twenty-two years old in 1975, and expect to earn at least middle-class wages during your working life, your government is counting on at least $289,000 from your pay. By contrast, a worker retiring in 1975 could not have paid more than $13,736 during his entire career (including his employer's share) in Social Security tax—an average of $30 per month for which he will receive at least $316 per month in retirement benefits. This is roughly equivalent to having compounded his tax payments by more than 7 percent annually during his entire working life—much better than he could have done on his own during the '40s, '50s, and '60s. Small wonder, then, that Social Security enjoys such widespread support among the elderly.

But who really deserves the accolades of today's retired population? The administration freely admits the system is on a pay-as-we-go basis—with today's taxes paying today's benefits—so it's obvious who's getting the bill. Do we thank the federal government, with its unlimited power of taxation, or do we thank today's twenty-two-year-old who, the first time he takes a job, agrees to pay at least twenty-one times more Social Security tax than today's retiree paid?

(There is no intention here toward depicting the American

retired population as undeserving of the benefits they receive. Anyone trying to live on the 1975 maximum individual retirement benefit of $3,792-a-year should be regarded with admiration. Most receive much less, and all live under the government edict which forbids earning more than $46 per week on penalty of losing what benefits they have.)

If it seems beyond possibility that a middle-income American and his employer could be liable for $289,000 in Social Security taxes, it should be pointed out that even this is a conservative estimate. The projected $289,000 tax bill for today's twenty-two-year-old is based on two very optimistic government predictions: First, the administration is hoping that cost-of-living increases in Social Security benefits will average 3 percent during the next forty years (less than one-third the increase level for the last four years); second, the administration actuaries will be held to a $289,000 tax bill prediction *only if* American wages rise no more than 5 percent a year for the next forty years. For the record, the Social Security Administration's computer analysis division has already devised and distributed (to government personnel only) a new tax projection based on 5 percent cost-of-living benefit increases and 7 percent wage increases. This projection would require $335,000 from today's twenty-two-year-old.

Even if we assume the lower 5 percent wage increases and ideal inflation statistics for the coming generation, the 1975 combined maximum tax of $1,650 is scheduled to reach $2,500 per year as early as 1982, $3,100 by 1986, $4,100 by 1992, and more than $6,000 a year by the turn of the century. Before he retires, today's twenty-two-year-old and his employer will be paying more than $17,000-a-year in Social Security tax. During his career he will have paid a monthly average tax nineteen times higher than today's sixty-five-year-old paid. And he will have been cheated.

The New Deal

It is August 1976 in Chester, Pennsylvania, as two men sit staring at each other across an open, sunlit square near the Delaware River. The two are strangers and make no move to greet, but they are connected.

Albert Gerard has recently turned sixty-five. After forty-one years with Bailey Manufacturing, forty of which were covered by the Social Security laws, Gerard has qualified for his $316-per-month retirement benefit. The checks began arriving several months ago and Al Gerard is quietly getting used to starting his days in Flint Square instead of the main assembly room at Bailey. He has time, now, to stop and look. The young man across the square reminds Gerard of himself as he was ("What was it?") in 1936.

Donald Eldon has just paused at the Flint Square bench. Eldon, at twenty-two, feels some urgency to move—anything that will help the days pass until he starts his new job as expediting manager at Bailey. As he stares briefly at the older man across the square, Eldon wonders if he were ever this anxious and eager to begin.

Gerard and Eldon have been joined together by the Social Security Administration. Their partnership, and millions of others just like it, is what the administration refers to fondly as the "compact between generations" which keeps the system rolling along. What Donald Eldon doesn't realize is that the compact has been designed to favor both Gerard and the federal government while he has been tabbed as the sponsor.

During his working life, Al Gerard always made enough to pay the highest Social Security tax the administration was asking. It was through no fault of his that the tax wasn't enough. His government was fonder of making promises than it was of imposing highly visible payroll taxes. Even if accumulated at prevailing interest rates, the tax Al Gerard paid would buy him no more than a $130-per-month pension—60 percent less than the $316 he now gets. By the time the federal administration could see that it had made too many promises to too many people, time was running out.

An attempt was made to take enough during the last few years of Al Gerard's working life to make up the difference. Between 1971 and 1975 Gerard and millions of others just like him paid more Social Security tax than they had paid during the previous years combined. But the tax increases weren't aimed so much at Gerard and his generation as they were at Eldon and his.

There is only one way to promise one group more than they paid for and that is by promising the next group less than they paid for. Albert Gerard was taxed for his pension during a time in American history when the prevailing interest rate was between 3 and 4 percent. His pension was computed as though he were being given 7 percent interest on his tax. Donald Eldon, on the other hand, begins his working career during a time when the prevailing interest rate hovers between 5 and 6 percent. The government promise to Eldon is based on compounding his retirement tax at slightly over 2 percent. It is hoped that Eldon won't see what is happening to him—that he will be, like all others his age, concerned more with his new job than his retirement, now forty-three years away.

Even if Donald Eldon did look into his future, he might not be alarmed. The Social Security Administration has planned for this and has published projected retirement benefits of up to $3,228 per month in the year Eldon is to retire. That's more than twice what Eldon is scheduled to earn at Bailey Manufacturing, so it sounds pretty good. Of course a pension like that is going to cost more money. Right? But, how *much* more?

Eldon and millions just like him would do well to compare deals with Al Gerard before they evaluate Social Security. Gerard paid his $13,736 at an average tax rate of 2.48 percent. He is retiring at a level at least 2½ times better than he could have done for himself. To pay for this Donald Eldon will pay over $289,000 in tax at an averaging rate of 6.4 percent. For this Eldon is promised a retirement benefit at least 24 percent *worse* than he could buy for himself. His losses, on retirement benefits alone, come to more than $117,000—which could have been in his pocket.

There is no question that a pension of $3,228 per month is a very good thing to have. To buy a pension like that, at age sixty-five, Eldon would need $358,666, which he could then give to an annuity company, bank trust department, or an insurance company. Any of these institutions would guarantee in writing to pay Eldon that much as long as he lived. But then Donald Eldon is scheduled to pay a lot of Social Security tax—worth a *lot* of money. Of all the Social Security tax we pay, the administration declares that 68.5 percent is specifically intended for our retirement benefits. That being the case, if the amount of Donald Eldon's tax intended for his retirement were placed in an ordinary savings account, it would be worth at least $475,945 * which would be enough for a monthly retirement benefit of $4,283—$1,055 per month more than the government is offering.

Here the administration refuses to argue. In response to allegations that our tax money could be doing much better for us, the Social Security hierarchy declares the point moot by saying we lack sense enough to save anyway. Paul E. Webb, regional commissioner for the Social Security Administration, was speaking to all of us in 1974 when he said that critics of the system "make the unlikely assumption that we humans, if we did not pay into social security, would wisely save our money or buy a private insurance policy of high value."

Whether or not it is in fact "unlikely" that we would spend our money as well as the government spends it for us, Mr. Webb's reaction remains a lot of paternalistic nonsense. If the administration is interested in getting the best for Donald Eldon, but simply

---

* To arrive at this figure, we have assumed an interest rate of 5 percent. Considering that the money is guaranteed to be left untouched for forty-three years, many banks would be eager to offer a substantially higher rate.

feels he won't do it for himself, why don't they begin paying him a fair return on his money? Does the administration believe that paying today's young worker 2 percent interest on his tax payments is the way to "wisely save our money"?

Someone will have to explain very carefully to young taxpayers how they can see their Social Security tax base leap to ten times the level of the generation before them, their tax rate jump 2½ times, and still end up big losers at retirement. When they realize what is happening they will have some tough questions to put to the officials in Washington and Baltimore.

As Donald Eldon pauses in Flint Square to anticipate his future and reflect on the old man on the opposite bench, he is unaware that Al Gerard depends on him. He is also unaware that he has $475,000 to spend on his future, because it's more than he's ever seen, and besides, his government has already made plans for the money.

Social Security's Life Insurance— The Price Goes Up on Unicorns

In the previous chapter we saw that Social Security's death-benefit protection costs a lot more than it's worth. First, because the so-called insurance price is much higher than would be needed for an equal amount of private insurance; and second, because the reductions, exclusions, and hidden taxes in the Social Security death-benefit system reduce its value even further. But since the time that Richard Williams died (1974) we have heard constantly from Social Security Administration officials about how "new, higher, contributions will mean higher benefits in the future." A short look into Donald Eldon's future will show what they mean.

Let's assume that Donald Eldon were to die in 1988 in exactly the same situation as we found Richard Williams in 1974. Eldon would be thirty-five, he would have paid maximum Social Security tax since he began work at twenty-two, he would leave behind a thirty-five-year-old wife, and two children aged four months and three years.

Just as the Social Security Administration promised, Eldon's family will get more than Williams's family got. Where Mary Williams and her children were promised total benefit checks of $213,762, Donald Eldon's widow and children could get as much as $493,385—a 135 percent increase in protection. On the other hand, where Richard Williams and his employer had paid $6,330 in Social Security tax by the time Williams died, Donald Eldon and his employer will have paid $34,390 for having worked exactly the same time. A 135 percent increase in benefits sounds pretty good until one realizes it took 443 percent more tax to buy it.

As was the case with Mr. Williams, Donald Eldon could have bought his family private protection, which would be worth much more to them, for a lot less than he paid the federal government. Eldon could have bought this 135 percent higher protection for $739 more per year than Williams's premium. Eldon's scheduled tax in 1988 is $3,430, which is $1,886 more than Williams paid. As bad as Richard Williams's Social Security life insurance turned out to be, he did much better than Donald Eldon will do. For every dollar of insurance coverage Donald Eldon will buy with his tax money, Richard Williams bought $2.35 in coverage with his tax.

Before Donald Eldon and his generation agree to pay four times what Richard Williams paid for "life insurance," it might do to ask the administration what is meant by "higher benefits" and "increased family protection." As a wise skeptic once advised, "They may be just raising the price for hunting unicorn, son."

The Myth of Inflation-Proofing

In the examples used in this book, little or no reference has been made to the so-called automatic benefit increases which are supposed to make Social Security payments "inflation-proof." There are four reasons for this.

1. Like all other aspects of Social Security, the automatic benefit increase is not a guaranteed right, but merely an intention of Congress, as was the 1935 "guarantee" to return the retirement tax money of those who died before reaching sixty-five. When this promise became too expensive, it was withdrawn. The object of the benefit examples used in this book is to compare public and private promises for value. To compare the contractual promises of an insurance company, bank, or annuity company, which can be enforced to the letter in court, with Social Security's promises, which cannot, is already unfair. Adding in the "inflation-proofing" at an unknown rate would further confound a comparison.

2. There is sound reason to believe that the current administration does not feel bound to "inflation-proofing" Social Security over the long run. In the State of the Union address given by President Gerald Ford in January of 1975, special reference was made to "the inflationary pressures" caused by programs "like Social Security." The president then asked Congress to "restrict increases in these benefit programs to 5 percent for the coming year." Social Security benefits were scheduled to rise at least 11 percent in July of 1975, to be paid for with an 11 percent tax increase in January 1975. President Ford did not mention scaling back the tax hike to match the maximum benefit increase he proposed. Though Congress can reject the 5 percent limitation on benefit increases, it is apparent that at least part of the administrative branch of government does not consider the "automatic" increase an irrefutable fact of legal life.

3. The method chosen by Congress and the Social Security Administration of financing its so-called automatic increases is so shallow an artifice, it does not deserve to be included in the "value" of the program to the public. In the case of "inflation-proofing," Social Security's pay-as-we-go procedure becomes pay-before-we-go. According to the complex but convenient cost-of-living increase procedure, the payroll tax hike for any benefit increase goes into effect six months *before* any higher benefit is actually paid. Thus, in any given year of a Social Security benefit increase,

workers pay taxes *higher* than the benefit level for as many months as the taxes match the benefit level, creating a float for the general revenue fund and negating the real tax value of the increase.

4. Congress may have no choice but to withdraw the automatic increase provision as it exists now. In spite of administration publicity, higher Social Security taxes are not needed simply to raise the benefit formula. What is changing slowly each year is the ratio of working-to-nonworking members of the American public.

Between now and the end of this century the present ratio of three workers paying taxes for every one collecting benefits will have worsened to slightly more than two workers for every beneficiary. Even if no new benefit improvement scales are enacted, those already passed, combined with a slowly worsening taxpayer/ beneficiary ratio, will guarantee a raise in Social Security tax every year. Therefore, while we can be certain of an annual wage base increase, the possibility of continually raising the benefit formula at the same rate is not as sure. The Social Security Advisory Commission, in its 1975 report to Congress, has warned that continuing the present method of benefit increases will add to the system's deficit, already expected to reach $7 billion in 1976 in spite of a 121 percent rise in maximum Social Security taxes since 1970. Given the inflation level and unemployment outlook for the next several years, it is unlikely that the present method of "automatic increases" can be maintained.

You Pay for What You Get—And What You Don't Get

Once the Social Security Administration decides a worker is "covered," he or she is covered whether the protection is needed or not. In fact, even if a worker could not possibly collect on his federal "insurance," he or she pays anyway. Whether Donald Eldon, or any other American worker, is aware of the fact or not, 68 percent of his Social Security tax is counted to determine his retirement benefit. Another 15 percent is used for Medicare protection, which will be discussed later. The remaining 17 percent of Social Security tax pays for survivors' and disability insurance of a unique nature. So unique, in fact, that much of the insurance is worthless.

Donald Eldon is single. The last kind of insurance he is likely to be interested in is term insurance for dependents, since this form of insurance is completely useless to Eldon unless he had a wife and children in need of support. Under Social Security Eldon must buy this kind of insurance, simply because it is in the package the system has concluded is necessary.

Social Security dependents' insurance is term insurance for two very basic reasons: First, it covers only a certain "term" of years—the years during which a covered worker has children under a certain age; second, Social Security dependents' insurance (like all the rest of the program) never has any cash value to the worker. If the coverage isn't used, the money spent for it is lost. This, of course, is what makes private term insurance inexpensive to buy. But even the most zealous insurance salesman would have to agree that term insurance for a person without a "term" to protect (no wife or children) is the worst way to spend insurance dollars.

Let's assume that Donald Eldon is twenty-five years old and has remained single. By this time he will have (along with his employer) contributed at least $7,600 in Social Security taxes. Should Eldon die at this point, all the money would be lost. A look at the "estate" Social Security has provided Eldon would reveal it to be the most worthless possible: (1) term insurance he didn't need, and (2) a retirement plan earning at a 2 percent rate with no insurance value at all unless Eldon actually survived to at least sixty-two. He would have died a victim.

Furthermore, the longer the federal government insists on forcing a single worker to buy coverage he cannot use, the more the coercion costs. In only the first three years under the system of "paying for nothing," today's young, single worker will have lost at least $608 even if he does live to retire. In another five years, Eldon's losses will have tripled to at least $2,131, and in another five years the losses will have grown to seven times the early years' level.

Keep in mind that the single taxpayer never has the right to ask that this "dependents' insurance" money be applied to his retirement benefit. He will get no more on retirement than the married worker who had use for the protection during his working life. If Donald Eldon were to retire at sixty-five as a single man, his total losses, from having been forced to buy insurance that couldn't pay off, would exceed $118,000 *—enough to raise his retirement benefit by more than $1,000 per month.

Nor does the single worker's financial beating end when he turns sixty-five. He will discover that the married worker, even if his wife never was taxed a dollar, is eligible for 50 percent more total retirement benefit than the single worker. If we assume that both workers paid the same tax, it is obvious that the single worker's taxes subsidize the married worker's benefit instead of his own. This loss is in addition to the $118,000 mentioned previously, since, as was pointed out, retirement insurance is figured separately from dependents' insurance.

It seems that the federal government's "compact between generations" is also an enforced compact between workers—under which the unmarried surrender at least half their Social Security taxes to the married.

Children—The Real Key

While it is certainly true that today's young singles are one of the prime financial sponsors of Social Security, getting married only rescues part of a worker's tax money from oblivion. To get what value there is in the system, one must have school-age children. Couples without children, or whose children are beyond school

---

* This figure is determined by compounding the yearly taxes spent, for coverage the single worker can't use, by 5 percent—the rate he could reasonably expect from a bank.

age, will continue to find that the Social Security Administration buys them the wrong kind of protection—or none.

To continue the story of Donald Eldon, let's assume that he meets Lynn Torrence and the two marry. Lynn has just begun a career as a nutritionist, and the couple decides to put off having children. The new Eldon family has replaced two single Social Security victims with one couple—slightly less victimized but still forced to buy insurance they can't use. Earlier we saw that if Donald Eldon died in 1988 with the same family make-up as Richard Williams, fourteen years before, he would have bought less insurance per tax dollar than Williams. But at least he would have left some immediate help for his wife.

If Donald and Lynn were still childless by 1988, Donald's death would leave Lynn no monthly benefits at all for at least twenty-five years, even though *both* of them had been paying Social Security tax for thirteen years to this point. The federal government sold Donald Eldon "children's insurance" (a unique product which pays off only when a worker has school-age children), when what he needed was life insurance, thereby wasting a lot of the couple's money.

In 1988 the Social Security tax level proposed for Donald Eldon is at least $3,430. Because the Eldons had no school-age children at the time of Donald's death, the money will have been horribly misspent. Mrs. Eldon will be eligible only for a widow's benefit payable no earlier than twenty-five years in the future. Unless she becomes fully disabled before reaching sixty, this is all she can get. Had the same percentage of Eldon's tax used for "children's insurance" (roughly 17 percent, or $583) been used instead to provide ordinary term life insurance, Mrs. Eldon would have been given the same retirement benefit that Social Security promises and still have been left with more than $62,000 in immediate cash. The remaining 68 percent of Eldon's 1988 tax was earmarked as his retirement contribution. This additional $2,349 could have been used to provide more retirement benefit for Eldon's widow, but was not. In thirteen years of work, Eldon would have paid at least $34,390 total Social Security tax, of which $23,557 (68.5 percent) had been designated for his retirement. None of the money was used to create the kind of insurance that would have helped a childless couple. Instead it provides nothing. There is little else to call this but fraud.

Remember that taxpayers don't have to be childless to lose Social Security benefits. It is only necessary that a worker's children be beyond their school years for the immediate life protection to melt away. This latter distinction makes Social Security much cheaper and less risky for the government to offer. For the vast majority of Americans, the child-raising years are between ages twenty-two and fifty-five. Nearly 90 percent of U.S. workers over fifty-five no longer have school-age children. It is also true that for every American who dies between the ages of twenty-two and fifty-five at least two will die between the ages of fifty-five and sixty-five. One more thing: For most Americans the highest earning years are the ten immediately before retirement.

Thus the Social Security system decrees that during the years when the highest percentage of Americans pay maximum taxes, more than nine out of ten have no life insurance protection. When the risk of dying before retirement is highest, Social Security is designed to pay off the least. As the years go on, today's young workers will see the real cost of allowing a bureaucracy to peddle insurance with a lot of carefully built-in blank spots. The price tag on the "zero insurance years" will skyrocket.

This time we will suppose that Donald Eldon and Lynn survive together until both are fifty-five. Donald's death now, in one of the blank years for Social Security, will leave Lynn with a lot of grim choices instead of protection. Remember, once past the years with school-age children, those under Social Security are considered "childless" whether or not they have actually raised children.

By the time Donald Eldon reaches fifty-five, the retirement portion of his Social Security taxes (68.5 percent) would be worth at least $230,000 at even a nominal (5 percent) interest rate. At his death, however, none of this money would be available to Lynn. Mrs. Eldon would be left with two alternatives:

1. Lynn Eldon could wait five years until she reaches sixty, at which time she would be eligible for roughly $1,630 per month in Social Security benefits. She would, of course, be subject to whatever earnings limitation was in force at the time. Since Social Security will pay nothing for five years, it is likely that Lynn will work and so lose part or all of her benefit unless she decides to quit her job. Keep in mind that Donald Eldon's retirement tax would by now have grown (with 5 percent interest accumulation only) to $293,545, which would be enough for a $2,128 lifetime annuity *without* any earnings limitation.

2. Mrs. Eldon could choose instead to wait ten years and be eligible for a Social Security benefit of $2,653 per month. Though she is likely to have retired from a job by this time, the earnings-limitation rule against this benefit remains in force until she reaches seventy-two. Ten years after his death, Donald Eldon's retirement money would have grown to $374,646, which would pay for a $2,997-per-month lifetime annuity, without an earnings limitation and without jeopardizing any of Mrs. Eldon's own income.

The choices available to Lynn Eldon are grimly tantalizing. If Mrs. Eldon waits the extra five years to sixty-five, her benefit improves by 62 percent. On the other hand, if she doesn't live to reach sixty-five all the money would be lost. The system that was supposed to be at the center of American security instead works like a macabre quiz show.

Compare the following with the pointless gambling of Social Security's "zero insurance years": Donald Eldon's retirement tax had grown to a value of $230,000 by his death at fifty-five. Mrs. Eldon could have had immediate access to all the money, which would be free for any use including an immediate $1,533 per month annuity for life. If she didn't want the annuity then, but felt she would in the future, Mrs. Eldon could let the money accumulate. The combination of normal interest rates (say 5 percent) and the fact that annuity contracts buy more for the same money as one ages would mean that each year Lynn Eldon chooses to wait for annuity payments to begin means an improvement in monthly income of at least 7 percent. If she dies before choosing to buy the annuity, all the money (as much as $374,000 by age sixty-five), instead of being lost, will be passed on to whichever heir she has designated.

It won't be bankruptcy that will kill the present Social Security system—unlimited federal taxing powers could prevent that. It will more likely be the discovery by large numbers of today's young that they are scheduled to underwrite their own destruction.

The American Working Wife—Gender of Victims

Of all the various segments of American society affected by Social Security, the most abused by far is the married woman who works. She is most likely of all to see her tax payments become worthless. The forces operating against the working wife amount to the grossest kind of bureaucratic male chauvinism. The rules boil down to two seemingly innocent principles of Social Security law. First, a woman is automatically considered to be financially dependent on her husband without any investigation of either's assets. Second, a worker entitled to two separate Social Security benefits can get only the higher one—even if the lower amount was financed with the worker's own tax money.

Like all the most popular forms of contemporary male chauvinism, Social Security's destructive edicts begin with the assumption of female weakness—and her need to be "protected" from it. Since the assumption is untrue, it becomes easy to pervert the so-called protection against a woman's real interests.

To some extent, the effects of the Social Security male-supremacy rule were softened in March of 1975 when the U.S. Supreme Court ruled, in the case of Weinberger *vs.* Weisenfeld (No. 73–1892), that a father caring for the dependent child of a female worker who dies is entitled to the same benefits as would be due a widowed mother.

What was hailed at the time as a landmark decision by the National Organization for Women, which called the ruling "a major victory for women's financial rights," was sadly blunted by later Social Security Administration interpretation. Stephen C. Weisenfeld had first brought suit against the administration in 1972 when, following the death of his wife, he was told that only his son, Jason, was entitled to benefits under Paula Weisenfeld's Social Security coverage. It was explained to Mr. Weisenfeld that the designation "father" did not exist in the Social Security Administration's lexicon of benefit categories. Only the female parent left to care for a deceased worker's dependent children was entitled to a personal benefit, the government said. This, Mr. Weisenfeld argued, violated the constitutional precept of equal treatment under law and the Supreme Court agreed.

The unanimous opinion of the Supreme Court with regard to Social Security's sexual bias was that "the Constitution forbids gender-based differentiation that results in the efforts of women workers, required to pay Social Security taxes, producing less protection for their families than is produced by the efforts of men."

Unfortunately, the Supreme Court left to the Social Security Administration the job of removing sexual bias from their rules. While the ruling seemed to be an order eliminating sexual inequities from all Social Security policy, the administration didn't see it that way. Instead of altering all sexually biased rules to conform to the equal-treatment doctrine, the Social Security Administration simply created a new and unique benefit category called "father's benefits" and left the matter at that. The other, far-more-often-used male-benefit categories were left untouched.

Thus, there are now three benefit categories for which a male married to an insured worker can qualify. He can be the "father" of his deceased wife's dependent children, the "husband" of his disabled or retired wife, or the "widower" of his retired wife who dies.

Amazingly, the Social Security Administration decided that

nothing in the Supreme Court's decision applied to "husbands" or "widowers," each of whom must still prove that they were supported by their wives to collect any benefits on their spouse's Social Security. No proof of support is required of women who apply for benefits under husband's coverage.

The reasons seem fairly obvious: If the male-support rule were thrown out in all Social Security categories, the newly created "father's benefit" would be by far the least costly to pay. In the first place, there are many more "husbands" and "widowers" of tax-paying American women than there are "fathers" of dependent children who survive their wives. Of these "fathers," still fewer could afford to leave their jobs to live under Social Security's current $2,550-per-year-maximum-income rule for beneficiaries.

The Social Security Administration estimates that paying the "father's" benefit in 1974 would have cost "about $20 million." Though seemingly an impressive amount, $20 million represents less than a single day's Social Security payroll-tax collection and will affect the system very little. Thus, it is only in the new "fathers" category that the Social Security Administration did away with the male-support rule. Removing all the sexual discrimination from Social Security, as the widely lauded Supreme Court decision seemed to demand, would have cost much more.

Those most often affected by this irrational rule are the poor. In households where a wife works to support the family while her husband draws unemployment or other kinds of welfare benefits, the wife's death poses an immediate crisis. The usual effect of the male-support rule is to assume that the husband was in fact supported by the welfare check and not by his wife, costing the family critical extra benefits.

It is at retirement, however, that women suffer the most incredible losses. Like all other workers, working wives have 68.5 percent of their Social Security taxes earmarked for retirement benefits. But before a married woman can collect her retirement benefit, the two-benefit rule must be applied—usually with devastating results. Every working wife arrives at retirement age eligible for two benefits—her own worker's retirement benefit and a wife's retirement benefit based on her husband's earnings. Even though both benefits have been paid for, we have been conditioned to accept that only one will be paid. The Social Security Administration tells us with their usual cheery sense of logic, "Whenever a worker is eligible for two retirement benefits, the higher of the two will be paid." There's that strange ring of benevolence again—as though we're being done a favor.

Actually retirement insurance is almost purely a savings function. The government takes money from our paychecks to which we are to have no access at all until we are officially retired—according to federal guidelines. Then, according to how much tax we have paid, the money comes back in the form of retirement benefits. Since the last three commissioners of Social Security have described the system as "an investment," the function involved must be saving.

Why, then, do we accept the deranged notion that whenever two savings accounts have been collected only one will pay off? If a husband and wife pay into two separate bank accounts, under two clearly separate numbers, what would be their reaction if a bank officer told them only the cash in the bigger account could be withdrawn?

The rule works this way: When a worker reaches retirement age, his Primary Insurance Amount is computed based on the Social Security tax paid in his name. His monthly retirement benefit is then either one of two numbers—his PIA or 150 percent of his PIA if he is married and his wife is also of retirement age. Thus, if a worker reaches sixty-five having attained a PIA of $300, he is eligible for a $300-per-month benefit if he is single or $450 (50 percent more) if he is married.

The economic rape of the married woman is best understood in the following example: The Sadlers and the Bowmans have been neighbors for twenty years, each couple having raised children and watched them scatter to other neighborhoods and cities. Ralph and Jean Sadler have both worked all their married lives except during the years when Jean stayed home to raise their three children to school age. John and Claire Bowman preferred to have Claire remain at home while John worked. The Bowmans also have three grown children. Now both couples have reached retirement age. It is early 1976.

Both Ralph Sadler and John Bowman have earned maximum PIA figures of $323, which allows each couple, since Claire and Jean are also sixty-five, a family retirement benefit of $484. But Jean Sadler wonders what happened to *her* retirement benefits from Social Security. Since she and Ralph both worked and paid, shouldn't the Sadlers be due a larger retirement benefit than the Bowmans who paid less tax? She inquires at her local Social Security office.

During a half-hour interview with a federal worker, Jean Sadler is told that her PIA is $154 which, in itself, doesn't surprise her. She usually earned less than half of what Ralph did and worked eight fewer years. Well, then, why isn't the $154 worker's benefit Jean Sadler paid for added onto the couple's retirement check? She is told that since her husband's PIA is $323, her "wife's benefit" amounts to $161 (50 percent) which in turn is more than her own worker's benefit of $154. So, she gets the "higher" wife's benefit and not her own. Then what were her Social Security taxes being used for all these years? She had been told two thirds counted toward her retirement. The Sadlers will get the same Social Security check as the Bowmans even though Ralph and Jean Sadler paid nearly 50 percent more in retirement taxes.

The fact that Jean Sadler earned less than half what her husband did merely makes the example easier to understand. Whether she earns less, the same as, or more than her husband, she will still be discriminated against. Let's say Jean's PIA had been $220 instead of $154. This would, of course, be more than the $161 "wife's benefit" she would be due under Ralph's Social Security and become the "higher benefit" in the government computation of their family check. But, as before, the lower benefit will not be paid and so the Sadlers' total check would be $543—more than the Bowmans could get on John's income alone. There is still no equity. To have raised her PIA from $154 to $220, Jean Sadler would have paid thousands more in taxes. She would have been taxed two thirds of the amount Ralph paid—a total family tax 68 percent higher than the Bowmans'—which bought her family only a 12 percent higher retirement check.

What the "higher benefit only" rule means to Jean Sadler is that in exchange for having worked most of her life, at wages close to her husband's, her pay will add less than $60 a month to the check she and Ralph would have received if she had *never* worked. More than two thirds of Jean Sadler's retirement tax has disappeared.

Even if Jean had earned a higher PIA than Ralph's, federal rules would work against her. Social Security law says that before a husband can claim retirement benefits on his wife's earnings, he must be able to prove that he is being supported by his wife. This test is even stiffer than the earnings limitation because a husband must prove that not only were his earnings smaller than his wife's, but that he has no other assets which he draws upon for support. None of this is necessary to be proved on a husband's retirement benefit. The government assumes that a wife has been supported by her husband simply because she is a wife.

The net effect of the federal government continuing its medieval concept of a wife being chattel—surely being supported by a man—becomes grotesque. An American male can add 50 percent to his retirement benefit under Social Security by simply producing a retirement-age wife, regardless of any other assets or means of support she may have. An American female can do the same only if her husband is willing to submit to a federal examination of his assets designed to prove he couldn't support himself alone.

The proportions of the rank discrimination against working wives are immense. Roughly 44 percent of the American workforce in 1975 is made up of families where both husband and wife have jobs. More than 40 percent of the total U.S. workforce is female. Nor is there any doubt which of the sexes is most affected by the "higher benefit only" doctrine. On the average, men in the United States earn 67 percent more than women while it is the female who leaves the workforce to raise children. The two factors combine to insure that a woman's pay will be worth much less in family retirement income, per dollar of tax, than a man's.

Beyond the obvious sexual discrimination of the "higher benefit only" doctrine, the rule tends naturally to redistribute money from two-worker families to one-worker families with little or no justification. In the cases of the Sadlers and the Bowmans, it's easy to see where the Social Security tax money is going. The following chart should help:

EXAMPLE ONE

Family PIA Earned		Family Benefit	Benefit-to-PIA Ratio
John Bowman	$323		
Claire Bowman	0	$484	$1.50 for every $1.00
	$323		
Ralph Sadler	$323		
Jean Sadler	$154	$484	$1.01 for every $1.00
	$477		

EXAMPLE TWO

Family PIA Earned		Family Benefit	Benefit-to-PIA Ratio
John Bowman	$323		
Claire Bowman	0		
	$323	$484	$1.50 for every $1.00
Ralph Sadler	$323		
Jean Sadler	$220		
	$543	$543	$1.00 for every $1.00

As the chart shows, the Sadlers' benefit-to-PIA ratio actually gets worse as Jean Sadler earns more money. The entire nation should be asking whether any welfare or fairness goal is accomplished by giving one-worker families a larger share of Social

Security taxes than two-worker families. Remember, the PIA is a very poor measure of actual income. Social Security is a maximum ceiling tax, which means John Bowman could have earned an average of $100,000 a year while Ralph Sadler earned $15,000 and both would retire with the same PIA, since both would have paid maximum taxes.

It is fairly obvious that in 1975 and 1976 a woman remaining at home after the children are grown comes under the category "luxury." The U.S. Department of Commerce confirms that, on the average, the husband whose wife can remain at home during his working life earns at least 4 percent more than the husband whose wife works. We should all be demanding to know, then, why families like the Sadlers should subsidize families like the Bowmans with their Social Security taxes—and why the American working wife's taxes should be tapped to do the job.

The Women's Movement would be very hard-pressed to find a better issue to lead their list of reforms in the years to come than Social Security. When Jean Sadler loses most of the rights to her $154 or $220 retirement benefit, the tax money lost amounts to a few thousand dollars. But today's young married woman in the American workforce is scheduled to pay for pension rights which will exceed $100,000 in real value before the turn of the century. Whether she gets her money or not depends on whether she chooses to fight or remain the Social Security system's single greatest victim.

Disability—The Crippled Coverage

The Social Security disability insurance program is of so little value to the American worker that we will touch on it only briefly— to list its myriad limitations. (Those who want a fuller discussion of disability benefits will find it in Book II of this volume, in the chapter beginning on p. 152.) For the most part, Social Security's disability insurance is coverage dragging a ball and chain.

In 1975 an American worker and his employer can be billed

as much as $162 during the year for the disability insurance protection of Social Security. The administration calls this part of the program "protection to replace family earnings lost when a worker cannot work because of disabling injury or disease." The chances that the program will actually do this are remote.

In the first place, the vast majority of injuries and diseases which actually do keep Americans off the job aren't covered by Social Security. What the system does "cover" for its $162 per year comes under the following rule:

> A worker must be unable to engage in any substantial gainful activity by reason of an impairment which can be expected to result in death or which can be expected to last no less than 12 months. A person must be not only unable to do his previous work, but must be unable to engage in any other substantial work which exists in the national economy.

In short, Social Security's disability coverage is protection only against wholesale disaster—at the price of much better insurance.

According to the National Safety Council more than 90 percent of all injuries which keep Americans off the job will last less than eight months. None of these people will have any "family earnings replaced." The same studies show that more than 90 percent of the injuries which keep us off the job do not leave a worker "unable to do *any* substantial activity." No lost "family earnings" will come to these people either, yet both groups mentioned are clearly disabled, and both lose family earnings. What they don't do is collect on their Social Security disability insurance.

Though at any one time fewer than 1 percent of the taxpaying public could ever qualify for disability benefits, some do get by the 100-to-1 maze of Social Security preconditions. This entitles those, now certified completely unemployable, to wait. The next barrier to disability payments is a five-month waiting period during which the government will pay nothing. Keep in mind that all those waiting have been rendered totally disabled and, under law, may do little or nothing to support themselves. In 1975 earnings of less than $50 per week could disqualify someone during his "waiting period."

The federal government could hardly have found a better method to sort out the "fakes" from those truly disabled. A worker, formerly the main support of his family, who can wait five months without any income, is likely to be beyond the category "malingerer." The gruesome fact is that the Social Security waiting period often precludes any disability benefit at all. A significant portion of those injuries or diseases severe enough to reduce a worker to complete uselessness "expected to last at least 12 months" will kill that worker in less than four months. Thus the family of a disabled worker whose injuries lead to his death will quite likely have been driven to a state welfare agency before Social Security paid its first dollar in death benefits. A single taxpayer could die, after battling eventually fatal injuries for months, without the Social Security Administration ever being required to issue a single check to anyone.

Moreover the bill for this battered level of protection will rise steadily in the future. An average rise in Social Security tax levels of no more than 5 percent will bring the annual cost of the disability program alone to $213 by 1980, $371 by 1990, and $575 before the turn of the century. Today's twenty-two-year-old can look forward to paying $1,678 before he retires.

The Phantom Investment in Medicare

It is beyond the scope of this book to discuss the medical merits of the federal health insurance program known as Medicare. Our brief investigation, then, will cover only the administration's financial sales pitch for Medicare—one of the most amazing offers in history.

Today's young worker is told by his government that an average of 17 percent of the Social Security taxes to be paid during his career will be used for his "Medicare coverage"—the medical/ hospital plan for his old age. Since all of us have heard grim stories of the difficulty in buying a decent health insurance plan once past sixty-five, the federal offer at first seems sound enough.

But we have to keep in mind that any offer is only as good as its best competition. Since the problem of retirement-age health insurance is really twofold (both being able to afford adequate coverage and finding someone who will sell such coverage to those already sixty-five), an "exclusive" offer from the federal government would have real value to the young worker. The point is that paying for health insurance decades before it is needed would normally be a poor way for the young worker to spend his money. But if he is buying an exclusive right to guaranteed insurability at retirement, his early spending is much more justifiable. That's where today's Medicare becomes a Mad Hatter's tea party.

The United States Medicare program is not an exclusive right of those who pay Social Security taxes. Any U.S. citizen, whether born in this country or naturalized, who is sixty-five years old can buy Medicare protection. He or she need not have paid any Social Security tax to qualify. As of June 30, 1975 the premium for both hospital and medical insurance under Medicare is $42.70 per month.

What coverage under Social Security does pay for is a reduced Medicare premium at age sixty-five. At present levels, the medical insurance portion of Medicare costs $6.70 per month and the hospital insurance portion costs $36 per month. Those who arrive at age sixty-five without Social Security coverage can buy Medicare protection for $42.70 per month. Those covered under Social Security need pay only for the medical insurance portion ($6.70), which is then deducted from their monthly retirement benefit check.

There is no attempt here to suggest that Medicare protection be in any way restricted. The present legislation, whatever its shortcomings, is a humane attempt at solving a genuine problem among the aged. The point to be made is that Social Security Medicare taxes currently being paid by the young worker do not insure his "right" to Medicare—he already has that right under law. What he is buying with his taxes is the future payment of the hospital insurance portion of his Medicare premium. This is, like retirement benefits, primarily a savings function for the taxpayer.

Looked at in this light, the government Medicare deal to the young worker amounts to the following: "During your working life, approximately 17 percent of your Social Security taxes will be used for Medicare. The benefit to you is that when you retire,* you will not have to pay the hospital insurance premium for Medicare. You will, however, pay, the remaining portion if you wish full coverage." As we'll see, this is not much of an offer.

Let's assume that the present $36 per month for Medicare hospital insurance will rise even faster than the administration predictions for average cost-of-living increases, so that by 1990 this premium alone would have grown to nearly $75 per month, to $122 per month by the year 2000, and a whopping $292 per month by the time today's twenty-two-year-old is ready to retire. To avoid this payment, then, would seem like a pretty good way for today's worker to spend his money—until he checks the price the government wants in advance.

In 1975 the Medicare portion of maximum Social Security tax is nearly $280, and is scheduled to grow each year. Under our present (and rather optimistic) wage and cost-of-living assumptions of 5 percent and 3 percent respectively, this part of the total tax would reach $370 by 1980, $492 by 1985, $643 by 1990, and so on—shooting past the $1,000-per-year mark before the turn of the century. The cost of Medicare insurance alone will reach $2,747 per year before today's twenty-two-year-old retires.

Since today's Medicare tax payments are extremely unlikely to benefit a worker before he retires, it is fair to ask how much the

---

* Under certain circumstances Medicare benefits are available to the disabled—after the five-month waiting period.

tax money would bring if the worker were paid a nominal interest rate of, say, 5 percent on his money—as he could get at any neighborhood savings institution.

Beginning such an accumulation in 1975, a "Medicare savings account" would reach $10,000 before 1990, and pass $25,000 before the turn of the century. Continued Medicare payments, at the presently proposed rate, would bring the account to $50,000 by the time today's twenty-two-year-old reaches fifty-five, $75,000 by the time he turns sixty, and over $110,000 by retirement age. This is the amount that *could* be available for today's worker to pay Medicare premiums at sixty-five if the government chose to pay a moderate return on his tax money. Instead, the Social Security system offers to "waive payment" of an amount, calculated to be $293 per month, in exchange for taxes previously collected.

Today's young worker should understand that $110,000, at age sixty-five, would buy him a guarantee of $992 per month as long as he lived—which would pay his Medicare premiums with plenty left for himself.

Some would suggest that the example used here is deliberately obtuse—that obviously Medicare taxes are being used to pay today's health bills and could not be accumulated as is suggested. Is it so obtuse, however, to suggest that when a government collects taxes "to cover a worker's Medicare insurance," as we are led to believe, that the worker understand that his taxes are worth at least three times the cost of what he's promised?

The Hidden Income Tax

Of all the abuses that today's worker has in store for him from Social Security, the most fraudulent may be the hidden taxation within the program the administration labels so proudly and often "tax-free." Here is governmental double-talk run wild. *The*

American worker is forced to pay income tax on the amount taken from his pay for Social Security. This is contrary to the most basic elements of tax law.

To be able to see through this particular federal fraud, we need to understand a little about the tax treatment of private individual retirement plans. Basically, there are two types: the H.R. 10 (IRS code 4019) "Keogh Plan" for the self-employed, and the Individual Retirement Account, or IRA, for the employee. Simply stated, these plans encourage a taxpayer to put aside money for his retirement by allowing him to deduct from his taxable income the money he sets aside. Not only is the money itself tax-free, but any interest the money earns while in savings is also untaxed. (For a more complete explanation of the IRA, see p. 139.)

These plans are not governmental charity. To keep its obligations under control, any government would want to limit as much as possible the need for welfare programs. The most logical way to do so is to encourage workers to save for their retirement by being fair about the way such savings are taxed. If a citizen agrees to put some of his yearly income where he cannot spend it (there are penalties for using retirement account money before retirement), the least his government can do is agree not to count such money as part of his available income for that year. The money will be taxed when it is finally used at retirement.

Compare this with Social Security. A worker earning $14,100 in 1975 would have $825 deducted from his pay as Social Security tax. The administration says that 68.5 percent of this tax is used for the worker's retirement benefit. The retirement portion of Social Security thus comes to $565 in 1975 for this worker. Like the Keogh or IRA plans, this money is unavailable to the worker until he retires. But when the Internal Revenue Service (who collected the tax for the Social Security Administration in the first place) looks at this worker's income, they will treat the $565 as though he took it home with him to spend. On a typical tax return, this worker will pay at least $113 in income tax on money he never saw.

With its characteristic genius for labeling drawbacks as "benefits," the Social Security Administration looks right past the discriminatory handling of retirement taxes, commenting only that "benefits are tax-free making social security more valuable than most private plans." This is nonsense. The proceeds of private insurance are also tax-free and, as we've seen, the contributions to private retirement plans are deductible. To fully tax a worker's contributions to his own retirement for over forty years and then announce, proudly, that when he gets his money back he won't be taxed again is not exactly giving anything away. The administration's battery of insurance experts know this very well.

The Social Security Administration's staff of actuaries must also be aware that even the benefit portion of Social Security is not "tax-free," as their spokesmen are so fond of chirping. The retired American worker, after having paid an income tax on his own confiscated earnings, now faces the toughest tax structure of his life. The benefits are anything but tax-free. The sixty-five-year-old will either pay a "productivity tax" or a "money tax," but he will not escape.

The "productivity tax" does not exist in the Internal Revenue Tax Code. It is the product of a web of other taxes and rules which render a sixty-five-year-old worker nonproductive—saying finally, "You must stop whether or not you are ready or else we will force you to give away your labor."

Michael Bennett has made the choice. Mr. Bennett turned sixty-five in early 1975 while earning $14,200 as a shop foreman for a small tool-making company. He was offered the chance to keep his job. Doing so, however, would mean that Mr. Bennett and his wife, Ruth, would not get any of the $484 monthly family retirement benefit he had earned by paying maximum Social Security taxes. He would continue to have Social Security tax deducted from his pay even though it would have minimal effect on improving his benefit. His income tax deduction would also continue. Finally, the choice became simple. If Michael Bennett kept his job and accepted all the other losses, it would mean working full time to bring home only $5,873 more than if he didn't work at all. In the space of one year, between the ages of sixty-four and sixty-five, Michael Bennett's net tax rate went from 19.7 percent to 58.5 percent. He chose to pay the "productivity tax" and quit.

Nor would a sixty-five-year-old need to earn middle-class wages to find himself suddenly in the heavy tax brackets. The rule is simple: In 1975, for every $1 more than $2,520 a worker over sixty-five earns, 50 cents will be deducted from his retirement check. If a wife is eligible for a benefit under her husband's account, but he earns too much, both will lose. Only earnings from labor are penalized—those with dividend, stock, insurance, or royalty income may draw all they wish without a loss in Social Security benefits. Earnings of only $5,000 a year after sixty-five would represent losses to a Social Security beneficiary equal to a 33 percent income tax. A $6,000-per-year income would boost an American sixty-five-year-old into the 37 percent tax bracket, $7,000 would mean a 39 percent loss, and $10,000 per year would mean 45 percent losses.

After a lifetime of accumulating retirement taxes on which he has already paid income tax, the American worker is told he must either live on the amount Congress has chosen to give him or lose his benefit. This is the system we are told is "tax-free."

Consider the future of the hidden income tax to be paid on Social Security. Today's young worker will see the retirement portion of Social Security tax rise to at least $1,500 a year before 1980, and over $4,000 before the turn of the century. By the time today's twenty-two-year-old retires, his retirement "contribution" will exceed $10,000 per year. Though the number seems almost impossible to imagine, by today's standards, only a minimal rise in the cost of living (averaging 3 percent a year) would demand total tax payments, for retirement alone, of at least $189,699 before today's young worker reaches sixty-five. Concealed in this amount will be a minimum of $22,000 in income tax liability, even if present tax laws are adjusted to compensate for inflation.

If we combine the information now known about the retirement and Medicare portions of Social Security, we can see that at least 82 percent of today's tax is performing what is essentially a saving function—money taken now to be used much later by the worker. By comparing the taxes for each with the promised return, we can see that this enforced savings is being compounded at roughly a 2 percent interest rate instead of what the present economy would allow.

The difference between 2 percent compound interest over forty-three years and 5 percent is the difference between $43 growing to $67 or instead growing to $143. When the $43 involved is closer to $200,000, the importance is greater still. Paying an income tax for this treatment would be laughable if it weren't so tragic.

Finally all invective fails: If the present generation of young Americans allows Social Security's proposed future to become reality, the level of economic rape will be beyond calculation. One is tempted to believe that the process will soon become so openly absurd it will be cut down. But this alone may not avoid tragedy. For if the federal government is allowed to gamble the benefits promised to today's retired on the demented hope that our economy will withstand limitless tax increases imposed on a working public who will remain totally uninformed, neither the young nor the old will be safe and in the end the generation of victims will be complete.

BOOK II
A Way Out

PART I

The New Generation Compact

The beginning of Book II marks the end of pure gloom and outrage about Social Security. Frankly, there is no longer time for these two reactions by themselves. If we now temper gloom with insight and are outraged only at a lack of action, we will find there are workable solutions.

Book II, then, is divided into two parts. In the first part, a major reform proposal will be presented. The plan is called The New Generation Compact and is designed to retain the single most important feature of Social Security—one generation using its power to help the next—while insuring that the transfer, instead of depleting the present generation, will make it stronger.

The second part of Book II is called A Survivor's Manual and is intended not so much to be read in a single sitting as it is to be referred to when needed. The manual contains a concise reference to current Social Security law as well as answers to the most often asked questions about the program. There is an explanation of the 1974 Pension Reform Act which gives important new protection for those covered under company pension plans. Perhaps most important is information on the newly enacted Individual Retirement Account, which for the first time allows an individual worker to provide for his own retirement—with a significant tax break. For those who need it, the manual contains information on how to decide intelligently on life insurance—how much you really need, what kind is best, and whom to complain to when something goes wrong. It is, in short, a manual for those who demand from their government a chance at handling their own future.

The reason we can be hopeful that prompt action will save the American Social Security system is that the present structure contains both the largest obstacle to reform *and* our greatest single asset. The obstacle is the vast unfunded debt Social Security has amassed, making a sudden loss of funds to the system completely impossible. The asset is the time left to the young worker along with his proven willingness to pay for what should be a substantial level of protection. If we can find a method of using the asset to do away with the obstacle gradually, protecting present beneficiaries while improving the promise to the young worker, the problem will be solved.

It must be kept in mind that the current Social Security crisis is not isolated to the beneficiary population, nor to a percentage of worker/employer payroll tax. The last five years of monster taxes for Social Security have perverted the entire American economy and to a major extent contributed to the current American recession. When $75 billion in potential spending power is being transferred from the working to the nonworking population, regardless of the motive, the ability of the worker to spend will be profoundly affected. When the money thus transferred does not stimulate the economy on its journey, but simply is funneled through a bureaucracy to keep an already low-spending population barely even with inflation, the total effect is still more profound.

Those who say the present inflation is proof the economy is overstimulated should be referred to a 1975 report by the Joint Economic Committee of Congress which concluded: "It was taxes, rather than the cost of food, gasoline, or oil, which hurt the average consumer most in 1974." Our most regressive, debilitating tax is Social Security.

Thus the situation which economists long felt was impossible

—widespread price rises without a rise in demand—becomes a reality. What *must* be the result of adding to the burden of those who are normally the spending power in the economy for the purpose of maintaining the nonspenders at a low level?

Though no one would accuse America's retired, disabled, or dependent population of being an unreasonable welfare burden, the method we have chosen to sustain them has exactly the same effect upon the economy as does the welfare system. The beneficiaries are correct in seeing themselves as receiving an earned right rather than welfare, but the grim fact remains that Social Security is so much unlike true insurance that its benefits take three times more out of the economy than all state welfare programs combined. We simply cannot continue to pay benefits by this method.

What would be ideal, then, is a social insurance system that could perform its function, which is at least 80 percent saving, through the normal private capital sources—and thus stimulate the economy instead of depressing it.

This ideal is possible if we are willing to meet our obligations to current beneficiaries of Social Security. This means that the changeover to a private social insurance system must be gradual. A $3 trillion debt, accumulated over forty years, cannot suddenly be added to the burden of the U.S. Treasury. Yet it can be conquered if we use our strongest national asset as the weapon.

The federal government currently has the legal power to sell a combination of life, disability, and retirement insurance to virtually all of America's young working population. With this power goes the right to collect "premiums," averaging over $1,000 annually, from the youngest, healthiest, and most able members of American society. According to surveys of the Institute of Life Insurance, this is two to three times more than these people spend on private protection. In short, the federal government, from the point of view of the insurance industry, is in an extremely valuable position with regard to being able to sell to the best American insurance prospects coverage priced well above the average.

The value of this government power to compel large-scale insurance purchase by the young is almost beyond calculation. The structure requires little if any sales force and almost no collection costs (the IRS "collects" Social Security tax along with income tax). Since the "group" is so large, no health screenings or medical check-ups are needed to guard against the bad risk. Finally, the promises made for these premiums are full of exclusions, exceptions, and averages. The "earnings assumption" to be lived up to is less than 3 percent. As "insurance," it is nearly ideal.

What would the private market be willing to do to obtain this power? For a chance to sell high-premium insurance to the best customers in the country—the young—would it be willing to improve benefits? tailor coverage more closely to individual situations? eliminate the "two-benefit" discrimination against women? do away with the earnings limitation? We can be sure that the right to be assured of sales to America's young is of such enormous value that the answer to all the questions would be Yes—and the commitment would be real.

Obviously the American government cannot casually transfer its right to collect taxes. Equally obvious is the fact that as ideal as the federal government's right to sell insurance to the young might seem, it does not exist alone. The Social Security Administration also "sells" to other age groups, not as ideally insurable, and because its internal structure is a crude "pay-as-we-go" system instead of insurance, benefit costs outstrip even the total of premiums. In 1975 the most expensive group insurance plan ever conceived went into the red. Taxes will fall at least $7 billion short of the amount needed to pay benefits. Yet inside is something very valuable and very profitable.

It is time for a New Generation Compact—a commitment made by the young to the old which offers security without financial suicide. The compact would involve the following steps:

1. Set a date no more than two years in the future at which time the major capital accumulation industries would be given a chance to offer a package of life, retirement, and disability in-

surance to those Americans about to enter the job market. Though some form of social insurance would continue to be compulsory, the new young workers could elect either the present law or the private offer.

2. At the same time, demand of the private insurers that for each young American worker who elects the new coverage instead of Social Security, they will acquire the obligation to pay benefits to one newly retired worker beginning one year later. The match-up formula would be based upon a maximum tax-to-maximum-benefit ratio wherein a single worker paying maximum tax would equal a single retiree entitled to a maximum benefit.

3. Regardless of what other inducements are offered to young workers to make election of private coverage more attractive, each New Generation Compact would contain the following provisions:

• Though the premium or tax for each plan would be the same for every worker earning the same taxable income (as is now the case), coverage categories for the premium would vary depending upon individual situation. Thus the single or childless worker would have a higher percentage of his total premium applied to retirement insurance in situations where his survivors' or dependents' insurance would not pay off. Within limits, he could elect the coverage he needed most.

• Once established for the year, the level of retirement insurance premium would be treated as a firm commitment of the taxpayer's income for his retirement. This portion would then be fully deductible for income tax purposes under laws already existing for Individual Retirement Accounts (see p. 141) and Keogh plans.

• No earnings limitation or other implied means test would be used to establish benefits. The insurance benefits (as opposed to those for retirement) would be based only upon the current premium, with no averaging of past premiums.

4. The opportunity to take part in a New Generation Compact would be available to any worker presently covered by Social Security so long as that worker is willing to waive his right to

benefits under the present federal system. Given the fact that the New Generation Compact would operate under standard risk insurance rates, this option is likely to be desirable or advantageous only to workers under forty years of age.

5. Those workers who do not elect the New Generation Compact would remain covered under present Social Security legislation, though a number of the proposed reforms (especially the revised tax status of the retirement portion) should be added.

Since the last two Advisory Commissions on Social Security as well as a number of other federal studies recommend that Medicare be removed from the Social Security system to be funded as a separate program by general revenues, it is not included in the proposal.

The concept of a New Generation Compact is designed to work with deliberate speed. The massive federal debt to be dealt with cannot be managed except in small portions. The idea, then, is to combine the shift from public to private financing of social insurance with a gradual phasing out of the present Social Security program over a period of years. This would happen automatically as more new workers are "matched" with the newly retired, which would directly lower the federal retirement obligation as each year passed. At the same time, a significant portion of those presently covered by Social Security would stay in the program with their taxes available to meet the transitional obligations which would remain with the government. While these remaining taxes would be gradually diminishing, as current taxpayers grew older and left the workforce, keep in mind that a much higher percentage of the taxes collected during this period would be available for dependents' and survivors' insurance than is now the case. Remember, much of the federal government's retirement benefit obligations would be almost immediately phased out, since more and more "match-ups" between new workers and the newly retired would take place year after year.

To see the mechanics of the opening phase of the New Generation Compact, we should look ahead at the first fifteen years of its operation. A large majority of the working population now under thirty (then as old as forty-five) would no longer be part of the insurance obligation of the federal government. Those now between thirty and fifty would have continued to pay Social Security tax to the federal government, but a much larger percentage of that tax would be available for dependents' and survivors' insurance. The oldest of this present age group, although transitionally insured by Social Security, would now be ready to be "matched" with a new worker for the same retirement benefits they would have received under Social Security. The federal obligation to this group as well would be rapidly phasing out. Finally, all of those now between fifty and sixty-five would have been "matched" and thus fully removed from federal benefit rolls.

As time went on a growing percentage of the U.S. working population would be covered under their own New Generation Compact, while fewer and fewer would remain the financial obligation of the federal government. Once the number of those promised benefits under the old Social Security program had diminished to an easily manageable debt for general revenues, the transitional phase of the New Generation Compact would be over. New social insurance agreements written after this time would be free of the burden of "matching" and thus could offer substantially improved benefits.

From the first instant of New Generation Compact reform, government financing of Social Security would change from a perpetual obligation to a specific and limited commitment to maintain the coverage of the present beneficiaries and the workforce (roughly, those over thirty-five) through their working careers. For those who remain in the present system, the transitional phase offers the federal government a unique opportunity to liberalize benefits. As a legislative problem, removing the most objectionable aspects of the present system (such as the earnings limitation and the two-benefit exclusion) would require a single, foreseeable appropriation rather than the far more agonizing decision to add to the existing tax burden forever.

Chief among the questions to be answered about the new system is whether or not private capital would be interested. After all, as valuable as all-inclusive group social insurance for the young would be, the obligation to pay one new retirement benefit for each New Generation Compact is substantial—so substantial that it would erode most of the early years' income from the new business. But the "match-up" chosen for the New Generation Compact (one worker in his twenties for one beneficiary in his mid-sixties) has been carefully selected and studied. There is profit potential in the plan.

The success of the transitional phase of the New Generation Compact is based on the great difference in potential life span of the two groups being linked. Remember, the New Generation Compact involves a personal match of one young worker for only one newly retired. Once the obligation to the retired worker ends (usually with his death), it is not replaced. Rather, from that point on, all money paid by the new worker is available on his account alone.

The probability that a person of one age will survive to a given age in the future is expressed, statistically, as "mortality." Thus the mortality percentage applied to a twenty-year-old male to express his statistical chances of living to fifty would be 90.2 percent —meaning that slightly more than 90 percent of men now age twenty will probably live to fifty.

Under the proposed New Generation Compact it is obvious that the mortality statistics of the new workers would be much better than those of the newly retired—at least three times better. What this means is that in a given sample of one hundred new workers "matched" with one hundred new retirees, at the end of the year the ratio of revenue to obligations would be changing in favor of the new worker. If we assume an average new worker, age twenty-two, then at the end of the first five years of the New Generation Compact, ninety-nine of the original new workers will remain, while eighty-one of the original new retirees will be left. As the process continues, by the tenth year ninety-eight new workers will be contributing, while sixty-one of the original retirees will be collecting benefits; by the fifteenth year the ratio will be ninety-seven to thirty-nine; and by the twentieth year ninety-five of the original one hundred new workers will be left, compared to twenty of the original retirees.

If we assume the usual methods of private insurers and other capital sources for financing debt as well as the current-return assumptions on premium dollars received, it is reasonable to conclude that the proposed New Generation Compacts will be generating net income between the seventh and ninth year, and will be operating at a profit beginning before the eleventh year of existence. At this point more than 89 percent of a new worker's lifetime premiums will remain to be paid.

Though this timetable may seem slow (it assumes a rather conservative 4 percent return on premium dollars), there are several reasons it would still be attractive. Most existing private insurance contacts do not show a profit during their first years. According to industry data, early expenses of acquiring business plus the need to establish legal reserves mean that the average new insurance contract isn't really profitable until the sixth or seventh year of premium payment. Thus the wait for the New Generation Compacts to attain profit status would not be novel to the industry.

Further, other aspects of the New Generation Compact could shorten the projected timetable for profitability. First, the expenses of acquiring business would be minimal. As long as many Americans would remain transitionally insured under present law, the Social Security Administration would be on hand to help with administration and record-keeping.

One of the major financial setbacks to private insurance is the cancellation of policies in their early years. Since the only reason for loss of business under the New Generation Compact would be either a company's failure to live up to a contract or evidence of a lack of financial soundness, most of the problem of premature cancellation would disappear. Also, the new proposal provides for a one-year period between the beginning of a new worker's premiums and the beginning of payments to a newly retired worker (not a gap in the retiree's payment, but a wait until the retiree is selected). Since the first insurance year for a young worker involves a minimal risk as well as no need for "matched" payments, it allows for the early establishment of a reserve which would further shorten the wait for fair profit.

More to the point of this book, however, are the benefits of the New Generation Compact to the average American worker, rather than to his government or private industry.

1. Though payment into some form of social insurance would remain mandatory, the possibilities for a more equitable and generous form of the system far outweigh this consideration. Once a free society has accepted the moral responsibility that genuine need must be met with fair welfare programs, those who are able to provide for themselves must do so in order to minimize the burden to others.

2. Even though present payment schedules would remain in force, the money would be used far more efficiently, making possible a much higher return for the amount spent.

3. The tax-deductible status of retirement premiums alone would considerably ease the present burden of Social Security on the worker. The transfer to a system of fully equal treatment of money spent would lessen the present regressive nature of Social Security's payroll tax.

4. The promises being made to today's older population would change from the hopes of a well-intentioned administration, subject to periodic "adjustment," to a firm contractual commitment, supportable in court, and regulated by the newly created federal Pension Benefit Guaranty Corporation. (See the material beginning on p. 146.)

5. The obligation of a social insurance program would change from a more and more oppressive and destructive pass-through of

the nation's wealth to a genuine savings-and-investment program capable of generating not only security but new jobs in a more enterprising economy.

What must be beyond debate is the need for immediate action. The current population balance between the twenty-one-to-twenty-five-age group and the sixty-one-to-sixty-five-age group makes this a uniquely opportune time for the New Generation Compact to work. Help for an economy that has been taxed into lethargy can't come too soon.

When the 1975 report of the Social Security Advisory Board concludes that we have "25 years to solve the problems" of Social Security, they are operating in a deadly vacuum. During that time the projected deficit in Social Security collections will have increased to more than five times its current level. We would be hopelessly transferring well over $100 billion annually from a productive, consuming part of the economy while accomplishing no more welfare good than keeping another part of the economy even with inflation.

The young people in the United States are willing to help the generation which preceded them as were others in the mid-thirties who supported the "Compact Between Generations" offered by the Roosevelt Administration. In order that today's young can keep that obligation without destroying themselves, they should be offered a New Generation Compact before it is too late.

PART II

A Survivor's Manual

1] The IRA and the New Capitalists

For millions of workers who do not have the protection of a qualified pension plan, September 2, 1974 began a new era in financial independence. Labor Day of 1974 marked the legal creation of the "Individual Retirement Account," a long-overdue opportunity for laborers to become capitalists as well.

The Individual Retirement Account (IRA) is a worker's answer to the kind of protection self-employed persons could set up for themselves in the past. An IRA makes it possible for you to provide for your future at the expense of the Internal Revenue Service. And, because of this, an IRA can make the difference between meager savings and maximized security at retirement.

With an IRA, you can deduct as much as $1,500 against your

gross income on your income tax return—and then put the cash to work for you. You must have at least $10,000 a year in wages to be allowed to start setting aside the maximum $1,500. But, even if your income is less than $10,000, you can begin operating with as much as 15 percent of what you earn. Whatever you begin with, you have already overcome the "participation," "vesting," and "portability" obstacles which many workers on qualified plans still worry about. For the money is all yours—and, if you're not around to enjoy it all, it belongs to the beneficiaries whom you name. While you are around and contributing to your IRA, your money may be invested in special, high-earning savings accounts, in insurance annuity contracts, in mutual fund shares, in common trust funds, and in any income producers that are acceptable investments for a qualified plan. That hard-earned cash of yours continues to earn more dollars tax-free, right up until your retirement when you begin to draw upon them.

Unlike corporate or governmental pension plans, you are not hampered by minimum age requirements to participate in building your pension bankroll; you are not limited as to what ultimate benefits you may draw from the IRA that you watch growing over the years; and you needn't worry about who is going to be appointed to wield your cash. You pick your favorite bank to play the role of trustee. Considering these facets of your IRA, you may indeed be envied by other workers who wound up under a qualified company plan, or by the governmental employees who are not permitted to start an IRA at all.

Your spouse can also set up his or her own IRA, and thereby increase the amount of tax-deductible money you can both invest for your retirement together. Through the separate IRA, your spouse can make use of income-producing investment vehicles different from the ones in your own IRA. While your IRA may concentrate on various mutual funds, your spouse could invest the funds of his or her IRA in savings accounts, certificates of deposit, or annuity contracts which provide a certain fixed amount of income. Thus, through necessarily separate IRAs, joint investment goals can be pursued in a balanced manner.

An IRA can be established as a domestic trust or as a custodial account with a bank as trustee or custodian. Incidentally, if the bank manages a common trust fund, your IRA can also legally invest in this, since a common trust fund is the bank's answer to mutual fund shares. Both mutual funds and common trust funds are legal IRA investments.

When you establish your IRA, the trust instrument with the bank or other organization must contain the following provisions in order for the IRA to qualify for the tax-free advantages.

1. Your interest in the assets in the account is immediately fully vested and is not forfeitable.

2. You are not to make contributions to the account in excess of $1,500 or 15 percent of your annual earnings, whichever is less, during any one taxable year.

3. You must not invest any part of the IRA trust fund in life insurance contracts, although you may invest in annuity contracts issued by an insurance company. You may also invest in endowment policies, but only that portion of the premium on an endowment policy which is for retirement savings is tax deductible under the law.

4. Your entire interest in the IRA must be distributed to you no later than the end of the taxable year in which you reach 70½ years of age.

Your employer, if he has not already established a qualified pension plan for you, can also set up a domestic trust which will provide individual retirement accounts for you and the other employees. But you cannot have *two* IRAs, one with your employer and one on your own. If you have already established an IRA by yourself, and later your employer begins an IRA for you, you will probably be able to effect a "tax-free rollover" of the assets in your personal IRA into the company plan.

Once your employer has initiated the domestic trust for the employees' IRAs, the trust may handle the combined assets of all the IRAs in a common fund for the benefit of all the individuals involved. But the employer must comply with the four already mentioned requirements for IRAs, and must keep separate accounting records for each employee in the plan. In this way, your employer has the legal and accounting duties connected with an IRA, while you have all the protection.

If you are managing your own IRA as a self-employed person or as a worker who has no qualified pension plan, however, you have the need and the opportunity to participate more actively in the growth of that IRA. You would be wise to consider the various ways in which you may invest the assets in it. In thinking about this, you will find it worthwhile to investigate the many and changing investment possibilities.

For the very conservative, there are government bonds. Besides the familiar savings bonds, you could buy some of the special United States Individual Retirement Bonds. These bonds do *not* provide interest income to you after you reach 70½ years of age, however. And if you die before that age, the government stops paying interest on these bonds five years after the date of your death. Neither are these "retirement bonds" transferable, and if you want to redeem them early, there is a penalty for doing so. When these features are combined with the typically low-interest yield on government bonds, many view the Individual Retirement Bond as a conservative security with all the qualities of an investment straitjacket.

Certificates of deposit, which pay more interest than ordinary savings accounts, provide substantially more freedom to manage your own money. And these certificates come in a variety of terms. They are available in 30-, 60-, 90-, 120-, and 180-day maturities, as well as in multiples of years. They are available at banks and savings and loan associations which vigorously compete for such investment money. And, considering the new $40,000-limit-per-account federal insurance, these certificates provide a solidly guaranteed investment for your IRA.

But as your IRA grows each year, through the contributions you make to it and the income earned on that sum, you may want to pursue a more imaginative investment course—especially if you are a younger worker. Indeed, many people are more concerned about trying to keep even with inflation, and they realize that government bonds and certificates of deposit have fallen behind in providing enough interest to match the inflation rate. We are thus brought to the question of the means somehow to share in the process which generates some of the inflation, with a view toward at least staying even with that inflation. This "sharing" in the process, as permissible in an IRA under the new law, can take the form of investment in mutual fund shares.

A mutual fund—more formally called an "open-end investment company"—is a corporation without a fixed number of outstanding shares which sells those shares to the public on demand and uses the cash proceeds to buy securities of other companies. The market value of mutual fund shares varies with the value of the assets inside the mutual fund. If the securities bought by the mutual fund become worth more, so do the shares of the mutual fund which owns them. Thus, there are differing quotations each day as to the selling or redemption price of shares of a mutual fund.

The "redemption" price is what the mutual fund will pay you for shares you have bought in the fund itself. When you sell mutual fund shares, you are selling them back to the fund itself.

There are many mutual funds—each with its own special investment policies. Some mutual funds concentrate on investing their shareowners' cash in steady-income securities, such as corporate bonds and debentures. Other mutual funds invest the bulk of their assets in companies whose shares pay a high dividend. Still other mutual funds buy shares in fast-growing small companies. And, of course, some mutual funds try to balance their investment program with a selection of each of these special areas.

You can pick from a large number of these mutual funds, depending upon which emphasis you want to pursue in your IRA investments. And you will be able to get daily quotations in most newspapers throughout the country, so that you may know every day exactly the value of the shares in your IRA.

Usually mutual funds pay dividends each quarter year. These dividend checks will be mailed to the bank which is the trustee on your IRA. And, if and when you decide to redeem the mutual fund shares, the proceeds of the sale will be sent to the trustee as well—for further investment. As your IRA continues to grow over the years, this diversified investment process, operating completely free of the income tax toll, can create quite a retirement fund for you. No doubt, in the years to come, we shall see new types of investments made acceptable for investing your IRA funds. And you may change your techniques and goals as you come closer to retirement age.

As soon as you reach 59½ years of age, you may begin to draw funds from your IRA. Only then do you pay ordinary income taxes on the benefits you distribute to yourself. You will recall how you built the IRA during these years, and how it grew, unhampered by large slices of taxes. You will perhaps find somewhere in the yellowing papers an old stub from your first certificate of deposit, or the bent business card of the insurance man who sold you the annuity policy. With a smile, you'll probably recall that mutual fund you're glad you held onto—and the other one you're glad you sold.

But most of all, you'll remember that on September 2, 1974 the United States Congress began to let you provide for yourself.

My old employer has refused to pay my pension claim. I had given up hope of getting my money without an expensive lawsuit. Does the new law help me?

For pension plans which already existed prior to the enactment of the new law, the regulations on your entitlement to a pension—or "vesting"—do not go into effect until January 1, 1976.

After that date, pension benefits to which a worker is entitled cannot be reduced or forfeited. Many workers in the past have lost their pension benefits because of long-extended vesting schedules or other elimination clauses in the pension plan. The new act, when it becomes effective concerning a worker's entitlement to a pension, eliminates such dodges and also requires that a pension plan pay all benefits in a joint and survivor form. This will prevent a pension plan from denying benefits to your widow when you die.

In the past no federal agency existed that was empowered to arbitrate pension disputes between employer and employee. As one Department of Labor official laments, "We would hear about the most flagrant rip-offs of employees imaginable, and we would have to turn these people away. Some employers knew very well that the people who most needed their pensions were least able to hire private attorneys." Unfortunately, however, these provisions of the act came too late for workers who leave their jobs before January 1, 1976. The Department of Labor, after that date, will handle such claims as yours.

I've just quit my old job and was handed a check for $1,257.00. Although I had never made any contributions, this check was money due to me if I left the company. Can I keep this money working somehow for my retirement?

You are in an excellent position to implement one of the provisions of the new Pension Reform Act—the "tax-free rollover." The new act permits, as often as every three years, tax-free transfers of assets from a qualified pension plan to an Individual Retirement Account (IRA). As long as this lump sum was paid to you within one taxable year, and does not contain any contributions by yourself, you may establish an Individual Retirement Account with the proceeds of the check. Furthermore, you will not have to pay taxes on the amount you contribute to your IRA, nor on any income it will earn once it is in the IRA, though you do pay tax on the money as you draw it out at retirement. There is, it should be noted, a time limit imposed upon this transfer of assets. The amount you received from the old pension plan must be transferred to the IRA (or to another qualified company pension plan) not later than sixty days after you receive it.

If the company I work for goes bankrupt, how can the new pension laws guarantee me the pension I'm owed by that company?

This question points up a very common misunderstanding about companies and their pension plans. It must be remembered that, especially since the new legislation, a company and a pension plan are two distinct and separate entities. There have been cases in which the pension plan went broke while the company prospered, and other cases in which the only thing left after a company's demise was the pension plan. Retroactively to June 30, 1974 the new Pension Act provides for the creation of the Pension Benefit Guaranty Corporation. This agency of the United States government guarantees you the pension benefits to which you are entitled under the terms of the plan—in the event that the plan terminates after the effective date. The Pension Benefit Guaranty Corporation is able to finance such a guarantee by collecting premiums from all qualified pension plans, and, if necessary, by borrowing from the United States Treasury.

Under my employer's pension plan, I don't yet qualify for a full pension—even though I've been working for the company for sixteen years. Does the new law enhance my position to get a full pension if I retire now?

Under the new legislation, you will be entitled to a full pension after only fifteen years of service to a company. But this provision of the new act does not become effective until January 1, 1976. At any time after that date, any employee with fifteen years of service to his employer is automatically fully vested and entitled to the full amount of the pension then due to him. If you should encounter any difficulties with your company in this question after January 1, 1976, you may register a complaint with the Labor-

Management Services Division of the Department of Labor, which is charged with the guarantee of this provision of the new law.

I'm not covered by any pension plan where I work. So what good is the new pension legislation to me?

The new Employee Retirement Income Security Act also provides some new breakthroughs for people who have no pension plan protecting them. Besides expanded possibilities under the HR-10 (Keogh) plans, a brand-new pension source has been created by the new law. This new idea is the Individual Retirement Account, or IRA. With this IRA you can set up your own pension plan if you are not covered by one where you work. To this IRA you can contribute—*tax-free*—as much as $1,500 per year. This money can be invested in mutual funds, annuity contracts, and certain government bonds, as well as in savings accounts or certificates of deposit at banks and savings and loan associations. All dividends and interest earned on an IRA's investments are tax-free income to the account. Only when you begin to pay yourself from the account at retirement do you pay taxes on the amount you draw from the fund which you have built.

If I need the money in my Individual Retirement Account before my legal retirement, can I get it?

According to the law, the purpose of an Individual Retirement Account is to provide pension protection to the worker who has none. The tax break given by the Internal Revenue Service on contributions to this fund lasts only as long as the fund remains intact. Any distribution or payout from an Individual Retirement Account which is premature to the owner's attaining age 59½ or becoming disabled would result in disqualifying the Individual Retirement Account. And if the account is disqualified, the Internal Revenue Service takes the view that the entire value of the account is then taxable as received by the owner. Even if you borrow money from the account, this disqualifies the account and the whole amount of the market value of the assets becomes taxable as ordinary income. Besides this ordinary tax, there would be a 10 percent penalty tax, which is figured on the entire value of the assets in the account.

I have already established an Individual Retirement Account, and my spouse, who also has a job, would like to make tax-deductible contributions to an IRA as well. Is this possible under the new pension laws?

Yes, indeed. If your spouse has an earned income, both of you can contribute to an Individual Retirement Account and both of you may take a tax deduction for the amounts you put into your IRAs. Each of you, however, must contribute to separate accounts, under the present regulations. But in this way you can set aside as much as $3,000 per year in tax-free earnings for your retirement. And each of your IRAs can have the other spouse named as beneficiary in the event of death. This possibility is one of the great boons of the new pension laws. Not only can a married couple get a healthy deduction—up to $1,500 *each* on the income-tax return—but the two IRAs provide an opportunity to pursue two different investment objectives. One account could specialize in securities while the other invests in annuities and savings.

I'm married and have two kids and my income is $15,000 per year. How much in taxes do I really save by contributing the maximum $1,500 to an Individual Retirement Account?

In this case, if you take the standard deduction on your income tax return, you would save approximately $330 in taxes for that year. Thus the $1,500 which you contribute to your own Individual Retirement Account contains $330 that you would have paid out to the Internal Revenue Service. In this way, you have turned part of your tax bill into an income-producing asset. For other persons making more money and paying a higher tax rate annually, the tax savings is even greater. A single person, for instance, who earns $18,000 per year and takes the standard deduction will save about $460 in taxes by making a $1,500 contribution to his Individual Retirement Account.

One particularly lucrative aspect of this new tax law is that it allows normally conservative "super-safe" investments to have much more investor appeal. For example, the $15,000-per-year family man can put his $1,500 to work for an out-of-pocket cost of only $1,170 (his contribution less the tax he saved). Thus even a drab-sounding 4 percent return of $1,560 in a year becomes a glittering 33 percent when compared to the true cost of investing.

If I establish an Individual Retirement Account, but then decide that I will take a job which offers a qualified plan, what must happen to the IRA?

The new pension laws do not allow a worker to be a participant in a qualified pension plan and have an IRA at the same time. Even if you stopped contributing to your IRA, it would still continue to provide you with a fund of untaxed money which, as a member of a qualified pension plan, you would no longer be entitled to have. If your new company plan allows you to transfer the assets in your IRA into your new company account, you may take advantage of this opportunity and thereby avoid paying the income taxes that would be due if you terminate the IRA by taking the money yourself. This continued tax-free treatment of your IRA funds is called a "tax-free rollover." But you must make this transfer of funds within sixty days after you join the qualified company pension plan.

In a couple of years, I'll be retiring with a nice pension—about $700 per month, which is quite above the national average. But this promise looks shaky, since the company is rumored to be going broke. What does the Employee Retirement Income Security Act do for me?

If your company's pension plan is qualified, the new Pension Benefit Guaranty Corporation insures all of your vested pension benefits up to certain limits. In other words, your pension is guaranteed up to 100 percent of your average pay in your five years of highest earnings—but with a present maximum of $750. This maximum guaranteed limit will be increased periodically with the rise of national wage levels. If your company continues in business, it will remain liable to the Pension Benefit Guaranty Corporation for reimbursement of pension payments by that agency to you. But even if the company goes broke, your pension from a qualified plan is guaranteed.

I'm just twenty years old. Since the new laws say I'll get all my pension benefits after fifteen years of service, does this mean I could work for three different companies for fifteen years each and then retire at sixty-five *with three pensions?*

You could work for three different companies over a forty-five-year period and indeed receive three pensions. You must consider, however, that although after fifteen years' service with one company you are fully "vested," you wouldn't receive nearly as much from any one company as you would if you had served longer. In other words, even though you were fully vested in a plan, you may not receive an adequate pension because your pension hasn't had very much time to build up. To keep a good man on the job, smart companies will show greater pension benefits to him the longer he stays with them.

I've worked for my company for six years, and the pension committee just announced a change in the eligibility, or "vesting," schedule. Under the new schedule, I must wait longer to become entitled to full pension. Do the new laws allow this to happen against my will?

Any pension plan may indeed change its "vesting" rules and scheduling at any time, with the proviso, however, that participants' benefits already accrued or vested are not reduced. For example, if you were entitled to half of what had been credited to your pension account, a change in scheduling could not result in your now being entitled to only one third of your pension. Moreover, if you have at least five years' service with the company, you may, according to the new laws, choose to remain under the vesting schedule which was effective before the change.

How does the new law assure me that I'll get the pension for which I now qualify?

Depending on the type of plan in which you are a participant, the new legislation provides much more assurance that you'll receive pension benefits than ever before. First, the administrator(s) of your pension plan must file with the secretary of Labor information about your plan, including a description of the plan, with continuing updated information as to any changes in its provisions; an annual report with audited financial statements; a certified actuarial report; and, if your plan is covered by federal insurance, an annual statement to the Pension Benefit Guaranty Corporation.

Second, your plan administrator must submit to you an easily understood summary of the same information on a regular basis, together with other, more frequent documents upon your written request. The law now provides more specific regulations upon the activities of "fiduciaries" who handle and manage the assets of your pension fund. Formulas are now specified as to the minimum contribution employers must make to pension funds. And finally, if your plan is covered by federal insurance, the Pension Benefit Guaranty Corporation guarantees you payment of your vested benefits up to $750 per month if your plan terminates.

2] *Social Security—As It Is*

Regardless of our intentions to unwind Social Security for a more equitable system, it will not disappear overnight. This chapter is included as a concise summary of what the system is now so that in spite of all the failings, we can at least take advantage of what is offered. The present chapter includes the Social Security structure as the laws exist for 1975.

Besides increasing the present benefits and providing for future automatic increases, the new laws also entitle certain individuals to still more Social Security benefits than ever before. Widowers from sixty to sixty-two years of age, as well as widows, can now qualify to receive benefits. Also, if a widow, or a widower, first becomes entitled to survivor benefits when at least sixty-five years old, she or he will now get the entire 100 percent of the spouse's benefit—if, indeed, the spouse received the full benefit. These new laws and amendments thus eliminate some of the discrimination between men and women in the calculation of benefits.

Retired beneficiaries of Social Security are now able to earn more than before without loss of benefits. These people may now earn up to $2,520.00 per year without losing any of their Social Security benefits. This, of course, means that the retiree may earn as much as $210 per month without any reduction of the amount on his monthly Social Security check. Besides this, the allowable monthly income figure is scheduled to rise in future years.

It should be clear from the foregoing that the most revolutionary aspect of the recent legislation in Social Security is the automatic increase provision which is present in the amendments concerning benefits and, as we will see, in the taxes to pay for these benefits.

To avoid irregular monitoring of cost-of-living hikes, Congress instituted the automatic feature, and it works in the following way: If, in the second quarter of every year, the cost of living has officially risen 3 percent or more over the previous year, then Congress has until November 1 of the year in progress to vote an increase in Social Security cash benefits—such as retirement, disability, and survivors' benefits. If Congress has not acted to increase these benefits by the end of the year, then the secretary of Health, Education, and Welfare will automatically implement the increase on January 1 of the following year.

Henceforth this process will occur each year, at the end of June. If, in any year, the June cost-of-living survey does *not* show an increase of 3 percent over the previous year, then the secretary of Health, Education, and Welfare will not declare any benefit increase for the following year. Federal price-watchers, however, forecast that it is extremely unlikely that more than two years will pass without *at least* a 3 percent increase in living costs. Thus regularly increased benefit payments from the Social Security Administration seem likely. And, of course, we can look forward to increased taxes to provide the money for these increased benefits.

Social Security—The New Cost

The new legislation and amendments mentioned above will naturally affect the amount of "contributions" which are also automatically deducted from your paycheck, as a glance at the little box on your paystub marked "FICA" will show.

At the present time, both an employer and his employee pay Social Security taxes of 5.85 percent each, or a total tax of 11.7 percent of the employee's wages. This tax rate is applied to the employee's annual earnings up to the maximum present taxable base wage of $14,100 per year. There will be further hikes in both the tax rate and the tax base, and these hikes will be calculated in accordance with rises in workers' average earnings throughout the United States.

In 1977, for instance, the total Social Security tax rate is scheduled to rise to 12.10 percent, half of which would be deducted from your wages, while your employer pays the other half. Again, in 1981 we would see the total tax rate hiked to 12.60 percent. And just five years later, in 1986, your Social Security tax rate would reach 12.90 percent.

Expecting a constant rise in workers' annual income, the government intends to continue raising your Social Security taxable wage *base* as well as the rate. This intention is very evident in that Congress has more than doubled the taxable base wage in eight years from $6,600 in 1967 to $14,100 in 1975.

In pocket-money differences, these hikes in the tax rate and the taxable base wage for Social Security mean that the maximum you could pay went from $290.40 in 1967 to $824.85 in 1975—a 184 percent increase. And, of course, your employer in this example must pay an *additional* $824.85, thus making the total cost $1,649.70 to "protect" you under Social Security for one year. And the next increase in the taxable wage base can be declared by the government at any time.

Social Security—The "Benefits"

We must understand that although the Social Security tax is compulsory, we must qualify to receive any benefits.

"If you are disabled . . ." Let us examine one of the cash benefits possible to the persons who have not yet reached retirement age: disability benefits. To a very large section of our population in the United States, disability and death benefits of Social Security are the only immediate concern, since these people are a long time away from retirement.

You can qualify for disability benefits under the Social Security system if you can prove to the administration's satisfaction that you are "unable to engage in substantial gainful activity." This translates into the reality that you must be unable to do any sort of work which would yield more than about $130 per month. By this, the Social Security Administration means that you are *not* classified as disabled if you can earn that $130 per month performing *any* duties. It does not matter if you cannot function in your accustomed job, but only if you can earn that amount in whatever activity.

In addition to this, in order for you to qualify for disability benefits, your disability must last—or be expected by competent examiners to last—at least one full year. Or the disability must be expected to result in your death. If this is the case, there is only one more qualification.

Generally you must have been employed and protected under Social Security coverage for at least five years out of the ten years immediately before you become disabled. However, many workers who are thirty-one years old or older and who were disabled after 1972 will need *more* years of credit under Social Security in order to qualify for disability benefits.

If you have met these qualifications, you may then begin the application process. You will be provided the various medical forms, which are to be completed by the doctors, specialists, clinics, hospitals, or whatever other institutions or medical personnel have treated your infirmity. These parties must then report their professional findings in your case, including such items as the exact nature of your disability, the severity of your infirm condition, the number and nature of the tests to which you were subjected, the treatments prescribed, and also their opinion of your ability to work in any job.

All of this having been completed, you must then provide comprehensive information as to your education, training, and work experience, and you must submit this information to the proper agency in your state which is designated to handle such disability cases. If, in due course, the agency's investigation of your case determines that indeed you are unfit for any job, and after the team of doctors at the agency have examined the case, your application for disability benefits may be approved.

There is a special rule which applies to those persons who become blind. If you become totally blind as delineated under Social Security regulations, you will not be penalized in the amount of future benefits you may draw from the Social Security system. In other words, as long as you can still work, even though you are blind, your reduced earnings—if any—will not affect the Social Security system's calculations of your annual earnings averages. Ordinarily these averages determine the amount you may receive in your retirement years. In this way, the benefits to which you are entitled are not reduced, as they would be for a person who is not blind.

The amount of your disability benefit check, if you have qualified to receive it, depends upon your average earnings under Social Security protection. The check will be equal to the amount you would draw if you were sixty-five years old now. The Social Security Administration views the applications for disability benefits as though they were retirement applications.

If you are under age twenty-four when you become disabled, you must have one and one-half years of credit for work under Social Security in the three years preceding the time of disability.

If you are disabled when you are twenty-four through thirty years of age, you must have Social Security work credit for half the period from when you became twenty-one until you were disabled. People thirty-one years old or older when disability occurs must have worked for five years under Social Security coverage out of the ten years immediately preceding disability; and these people must also be "fully insured," i.e., they must have worked enough under Social Security to be eligible for retirement benefits.

A disabled worker's wife also qualifies for benefits if she is at least sixty-two years old, or if she is caring for a child under eighteen years of age, or if that child is disabled before age twenty-two. These children are also eligible for benefits themselves, as are any children of disabled workers as long as the children are still in school from eighteen through twenty-two years of age.

Also a disabled worker's wife may receive as much as one half of the amount of the worker's benefits. The worker's children who qualify may also receive half of the worker's primary benefits as well. However, the worker's wife may receive a reduced benefit check if she applies for it before she reaches sixty-five years of age, unless a child under eighteen or disabled before twenty-two is under her care. In these cases, it should be noted that a child "disabled before age 22," and under the care of the worker's wife, must be a person who is not able to live independently. In actual cases, it is evident that this means disabled to the degree that he or she requires to be fed and dressed.

The widow of a deceased worker who would have qualified for Social Security retirement benefits may herself qualify for disability benefits as early as fifty years of age, but only if she is severely disabled. Usually a disabled widow qualifies for Social Security benefits only if her disability occurred before or within seven years of her husband's death or within seven years of her receipt of her mother's benefits.

But if the widow was receiving benefits as a widow with children under her care following the death of the insured worker, she could be entitled to disability payments herself. Her disability, however, would have to have begun within seven years after her mother's benefits ended. Her benefit payment would amount to from 50 percent to 71.5 percent of her deceased husband's primary amount. The precise amount would depend upon the widow's age at the time she became entitled to Social Security benefits as a disabled widow.

Someone who becomes disabled before reaching the age of twenty-two may receive disability benefits if one of his parents either receives disability or retirement benefit payments or dies after having worked sufficient time under Social Security coverage.

"For the Survivors..." The family of a worker protected under Social Security may be entitled to survivors' benefits if the worker dies while insured under the system—regardless of his age at the time of death. He must, however, be "fully insured" to guarantee survivors' benefits for his dependent parents, who must be sixty-two years old or older. If the deceased worker was in a job protected by Social Security for at least half of the three years immediately previous to his death, then his children and their mother may be entitled to partial benefits as survivors.

Under the present program of Social Security, survivors' benefits may be paid to a widow at any age if she is caring for children under eighteen or for any older disabled child who qualifies for benefits. She also may receive benefits if her children are under twenty-two years of age and are still in school. Dependent, unmarried children who are under eighteen, or, if they are in school, under twenty-two years of age, may also qualify for survivors' benefits, as well as any disabled children eighteen years old and older, providing their disability started before age twenty-two.

Others who may qualify for survivors' benefits include your parents, with the proviso that they are at least sixty-two years old and are dependent upon you at the time of your death. Your divorced wife may even be entitled to survivors' benefits if the marriage lasted twenty years.

Your widow, even if she remarries after she attains sixty years of age, may still be entitled to survivors' benefits. This rule also applies to dependent widowers after they reach age sixty. The survivors' benefits in such cases will amount to half of the retirement check due to the deceased spouse. Your widow, if she remarries, may also be eligible to a wife's benefit under her new spouse's Social Security coverage. If so, your widow could not get both checks, but only the larger of the two. If your widow became eligible for Social Security survivors' payments upon attaining sixty-five years of age or after, but you had taken a reduced benefit by retiring between the ages of sixty-two and sixty-five, she would receive only what you would be receiving if you were still alive. Or if she became eligible before she attained sixty-five years of age, and you would have been getting reduced benefits if still alive, your widow would get either that reduced amount or the benefit payable to you at age sixty-five, but reduced for her age of entitlement—whichever sum is less.

Under the laws now in effect, if your widow first became eligible for benefits at sixty-five or older—and if you never got reduced benefits before you were sixty-five—she may now get 100 percent of the unreduced benefits due you at age sixty-five. However, even if you never got reduced benefits before you reached sixty-five, but she became eligible *before* she was sixty-five, she will get reduced benefits according to her age when she becomes eligible.

Your widow, if she is younger than sixty years of age, may get benefit checks if she is caring for unmarried children under age eighteen, or for a disabled child eighteen years old or older whose disability began before age twenty-two. As the mother of the child or children, your widow would receive 75 percent of the benefits you would be getting if you had retired at sixty-five—this latter benefit is called the "primary amount." But, this payment stops when the youngest child attains eighteen years of age, unless she has a disabled child in her care. And once these payments stop, your widow cannot get survivors' benefits until she reaches sixty and has still not remarried. Only in the event of her being disabled would she begin receiving survivors' benefits at fifty years of age.

As should be obvious, the Social Security regulations for widows' entitlement to benefits vary with circumstances. A widow without children may collect survivors' benefits only if her husband was "fully insured" under Social Security. But a widow with a disabled child, or a child under eighteen, may get survivors' benefit payments if her husband was either "fully insured" or "currently insured." The deceased husband, in order to be "currently insured," must have logged at least one and one-half years of work credit under Social Security within the three years immediately preceding his death.

Under the present legislation, even your divorced widow may be entitled to receive survivors' benefits if she is at least sixty years old (or fifty years old if disabled) and if she was married to you for a minimum of twenty years before the divorce. She might also qualify for benefits before she becomes sixty years old if she is caring for your children who are less than eighteen years old, or were disabled before age twenty-two. But she cannot get any payments if your children in her care are students of eighteen through twenty-two years of age.

Now, if at the time of your death, you are either "fully insured" or "currently insured" under Social Security, then each of your surviving children is eligible to 75 percent of your primary retirement benefit amount. Children may become entitled to benefits when either their father or their mother dies.

But there is a limit upon the benefits that one family may receive from the Social Security Administration in any one month. This limit varies, depending upon the deceased worker's average earnings under Social Security coverage. Usually the total benefit amount payable to a widow with one child cannot exceed the family maximum amount. If she cares for two dependent children, however, even though she and the children are owed more than the family limit, the Social Security Administration reduces the benefits so as not to exceed the family limit.

Your parents may be able to get benefits when you die, but they both must be at least sixty-two years old and they must have been getting at least half their support from you before you died. You must be "fully insured" in this case of death, or there will be no survivors' benefits for them under Social Security. If both parents are eligible, each would receive 75 percent of your primary retirement benefits. But if there is only one such parent who qualifies, he or she would get 82½ percent of your primary retirement benefits.

In accordance with the new legislation, if a widower wants to qualify for survivors' benefit payments, he must be at least sixty years old and must have been dependent upon his wife for more than half of his support, and she must also have been "fully insured" under Social Security. The amount of the check he would get is variable, depending upon his age when he makes a claim.

Except in the event when they are the parents of a child, the spouse of a qualified worker who has died cannot receive benefit payments as a survivor until their marriage has been in effect for nine months. If, however, the qualified worker died as the result of an accident, then payments may be made providing the marriage had been in effect for a minimum of three months.

If you were born before 1930 and you die, monthly survivors' benefit checks can be paid to certain members of your family even if you have only one quarter (three months) of Social Security coverage for each year after 1950 and up to the year of your death. But if you were born in 1930 or later, you must have one quarter of coverage for each year after you reached twenty-one years of age, until the time of your death.

When a worker covered by Social Security dies, there becomes available a lump-sum death benefit. This benefit amount is equivalent to three times the worker's primary benefit, but with a maximum of $255. This lump sum is paid to the worker's surviving spouse if it is claimed, but only providing that the spouse was living with the insured worker at the time of death.

If there is no surviving spouse, arrangements can be made

by others to pay the benefit to a third person who has paid the worker's funeral expenses.

"For the golden years . . ." If you are planning to work after the authorized retirement age of sixty-five, you should still apply for benefits three to six months before attaining sixty-five years of age. The new laws state that if you delay your retirement, you can get an increase in retirement benefits of 1 percent for each year you forestall your retirement between the official, authorized retirement age and seventy-two years of age. By applying early, even though you are not planning to retire soon, your rights to increased benefits by further earnings are not affected. Besides this optional ability to increase your benefits, we must also recall that all retirement benefit payments to workers under Social Security will, in the present official view, rise steadily and automatically in accordance with the 1972 legislation.

When you do begin to draw retirement benefit checks, under the present law, your wife and children may also qualify to do so. Your wife must be at least sixty-two to receive benefits—or she must be caring for an unmarried child under eighteen or a child disabled before age twenty-two. And such children are also eligible for monthly benefit checks, as are those children under the age of twenty-two and who are still in school.

Your wife, if she has reached sixty-five years of age, would get one half of your primary retirement benefit, which is the amount due you if you begin to draw retirement checks when you reach age sixty-five. Each of your children can also draw 50 percent of your primary retirement benefit amount, if they qualify. But the family limitation on the total which one family may receive is the controlling factor. No family may draw more than $828.30 per month in Social Security benefits, counting all possible claims. This present maximum family amount will also increase whenever the Social Security benefits automatically increase as a whole. But few families ever receive the full maximum benefit.

Even the grandchild of a worker or of the worker's spouse

may be eligible for benefits under the present retirement provisions in the new law. If the grandchild has been living with and receiving at least one half of his support from the worker who is his grandparent, the grandchild may qualify to receive benefits—provided only, however, that the grandchild has been living with the grandparent for one year *before* the grandparent becomes eligible for retirement benefits. The grandchild may also qualify for benefits if he began living with the worker before that grandchild reached eighteen years of age.

The divorced wife of a now retired worker may be eligible for monthly retirement benefits if she is sixty-two years old or older and if she was married to the worker for twenty years. But if she remarries, she is no longer eligible for benefits related to those of her first husband. Payments may, however, continue to any children of that first husband who are in her care.

A husband dependent upon a retired female worker may be eligible for benefits if he is at least sixty-two years old and depends upon her for at least one half of his support.

How do I know if I'm "fully insured" under Social Security now?

You are "fully insured" if you have worked for at least three months out of each calendar year since 1950 and have had Social Security taxes taken out of your earnings during all those periods. You are also "fully insured" if you have worked under Social Security coverage for at least three months out of each calendar year since you became twenty-one, and prior to the year you become sixty-two or die. These three-month periods are called "quarters of coverage." No one can be fully insured if he has less than six quarters of coverage to his credit. And if you have forty quarters of coverage, you are fully insured for life. In figuring the number of calendar years in which you have at least one quarter of coverage, do *not* count any year during which you were disabled.

A "fully insured" status, however, is only *one* requirement for determining whether or not a particular type of benefit will be paid to you. It does *not* mean that all types of Social Security benefits are payable to you, nor does it have much to do with the amount of benefits that may be paid to you.

Why, under Social Security laws, is it sometimes better for retired people to live together rather than get married?

Many retired couples have found that, as recipients of Social Security benefit checks, getting married results in a cut in their combined benefits. Such a couple becomes aware that, if they do marry, they must notify the Social Security Administration of their "change in status" which, under the present laws, will result in the reduction or the elimination of the woman's benefits. Any widow who is less than sixty years old, for example, would lose her survivors' benefits under the Social Security system if she remarries. Also, a widower who was previously classified as dependent may lose his benefits. Since an increasing percentage of retired people exist on Social Security income exclusively, formal marriage is often economically out of the question.

How can I prove my age to the Social Security office if I cannot find or do not have a birth certificate?

Many U.S. citizens and even more foreign-born workers have this problem, and in order to avoid delays in applying or receiving benefits, you must substitute other proofs of age. Military service records, draft cards, discharge papers, school records, and even baptismal certificates can all help to verify your age for Social Security purposes. All documents which show your date of birth will aid you in corroborating your claim. Census records, insurance policies, marriage certificates, labor union records, passports, old voter's registration cards, and the birth certificates of your child or children are helpful to establish your age. These will be used in conjunction with the Social Security Administration's own records on you to substantiate your age. Generally, any copies of official documents which you submit should be certified as genuine by the official issuing them. Even documents in foreign languages can be submitted, since the Social Security Administration has access to United States government translators.

If I retire to live in another country, do I still qualify to receive Social Security retirement benefit checks?

Providing you do not choose to retire in Albania, North Korea, Vietnam, Cuba, Communist China, or in the Soviet-occupied zones of Germany and Berlin, you can receive your monthly Social Security retirement checks at your foreign address. Indeed, many thousands of Americans who want to take advantage of lower living costs have their retirement homes outside the United States borders. Mexico, for example, has a large contingent of American retirees who are able to increase the buying power of their Social Security checks due to lower food, clothing, and housing costs. And Costa Rica is also very cordial to retired Americans.

All that is necessary, once you have qualified for receiving retirement benefit checks, is to inform the Social Security Administration when you change your address. Thus you will be assured of your monthly checks without interruption. Depending upon where you make your retirement home, you may even be able to put into savings a part of your monthly Social Security check.

How long must I wait for benefits from Social Security if I become disabled?

The minimum clerical processing time for a disability claim is ninety days, on the average, from the date that you file until you would receive any benefit check. There is, however, a five-month waiting period from the exact date the disability is deemed to have occurred. Thus to begin getting benefit checks as early as possible, you should begin the filing procedure soon after the day of the disabling injury—certainly within the following month. If you let more than two months pass without filing a claim for disability benefits, the three-month processing period will extend the time you must wait before you begin receiving benefit checks.

The aforementioned process, of course, is what the system should be. Social Security officials have admitted that *eight* months often slip by before a disability claimant receives his first benefit check. So file early and keep checking with the representative handling your case.

How do I get a refund from the Social Security Administration if, by working extra jobs, I and my additional employers "overcontribute" to Social Security?

Even though you, as an employee, have overpaid the maximum amount to be taken from your earnings, you must wait until you file regular income tax return 1040 to file for a refund of your excess Social Security contributions. This refund, of course, bears no interest to you from the government. Your refund, however, usually becomes a credit entry on your tax form, to be applied against the income tax you owe the Internal Revenue Service. If you are not required to file an income tax return for the year, you should request your refund of Social Security contributions on form 843, which is obtainable at your local Social Security branch office.

Your employers, however, have no rights or power to get any refund or tax credit whatsoever upon what they have paid in by overcontributing. These monies are forfeited to the government and are not in any way credited to your own Social Security record.

Can I find out exactly how much the Social Security system owes me right now?

You cannot find out how much the Social Security Administration "owes" you unless you are faced with a specific event which may be covered by the many Social Security regulations. You can, of course, request a statement of your earnings, as interpreted by the administration, by obtaining and completing the request form which is available from your Social Security branch office. But this statement is merely the basic calculation upon which it is necessary to compute the specific amount of benefits payable to you in a wide variety of events and conditions. That is, you are "owed" benefits only if you qualify; and, if you do, the specific amount of the benefit check is to be computed on the statement of earnings covered under Social Security. Such amount of benefit checks may increase or decrease as time goes on, and is an entirely different amount than would be "owed" to you at another time, under different conditions.

If my employer goes bankrupt, and it is discovered that he has not paid any Social Security contributions on my behalf for many months, am I insured?

As long as deductions were taken from your earnings for the purpose of making contributions to Social Security, your coverage remains in force. In this case, the responsibility for the payment would be upon your employer and, if he has not forwarded these contributions of yours to the Social Security Administration, agents of the Internal Revenue Service have their methods of collecting this tax as they would any other.

What documents must I show to the Social Security office if I want to apply for disability benefits?

You must present medical evidence of your mental or physical impairment, including: (1) a report signed by a licensed physician; (2) a copy of medical records, if any, from a hospital, clinic, sanatorium, or institution; (3) and any other medical evidence which would help prove your impairment, such as clinical or laboratory findings, results of examinations, diagnoses, treatments applied, and prescriptions.

If I never had a job, or never worked under Social Security coverage, do I qualify for any benefits?

You would not qualify for any Social Security benefits unless you are over seventy-two years of age, or unless you are a dependent of a worker who has worked under Social Security. A wife who has never worked under Social Security, for example, could become eligible for benefits. But this would be the case only if her spouse is entitled to draw benefits should he retire, become disabled, or die. In the latter case, the widow would receive benefits even though she had not worked to obtain Social Security coverage.

If I, as a retired or disabled person, take a large profit on the sale of my house, or on the sale of some securities, can this affect my claim to Social Security benefits?

Unless you are a real estate broker or a securities broker or dealer, the occasional capital gain on the sale of real or personal property will not affect your claims to Social Security benefit payments. As a general rule, only income earned from personal labor affects Social Security benefits.

APPENDIX A

What the Future Will Cost

In order to provide for your own future you must know how long a particular sum of money will last. Since most family budgets are figured monthly, it would help to know how long a sum of money could continue to provide monthly income—assuming some interest factor. To use the following chart, first determine how many *years* you would like *monthly* income to last. Read down the chart until you come to the proper line under the column "Years." Then read across this line to the interest factor which you are *certain* a sum of money will earn while you use it for monthly income. The number you find under the chosen interest factor on the proper line is the amount necessary to provide $1 per month for the number of years you indicated. *Example One:* If you want to guarantee yourself $200 per month for fifteen years, the chart will show what such a guarantee costs. Read down the "Years" column to "15" and across to the "5%" column (most savings-and-loan accounts guarantee at least 5 percent). The number you find is 126. Multiply 126 by the amount you wish to pay yourself over the fifteen years—$200—and you get $25,200. Thus, if you have $25,200 to invest at 5 percent, you may deduct $200 per month every month for fifteen years before the money runs out. *Example Two:* If you already have a sum of money and want to know how long it will last if paid to you monthly, simply find the right factor (under the interest column on the appropriate year line) and *divide* it by the amount you have. By this method, if you have $10,000 and you wish to pay yourself for ten years at 5 percent divide the ten-year/5 percent factor (94) by $10,000. The result is $106 per month.

Years	3%	3½ %	4%	4½ %	5%	5½ %	6%
1	12	12	12	12	12	12	12
2	23	23	23	23	23	23	23
3	34	34	34	34	33	33	33
4	45	45	44	44	43	43	43
5	56	55	54	54	53	52	52
6	66	65	64	63	62	61	60
7	76	74	73	72	71	70	68
8	85	84	82	80	79	78	76
9	95	93	91	89	87	85	83
10	104	101	99	96	94	92	90
11	112	109	107	104	101	99	96
12	121	117	114	111	108	105	102
13	129	125	121	118	115	111	108
14	137	133	128	124	121	117	113
15	145	140	135	131	126	122	119
16	152	147	142	137	132	128	123
17	160	154	148	142	137	132	128
18	167	160	154	148	142	137	132
19	174	166	160	153	147	141	136
20	180	172	165	158	152	145	140
21	187	178	170	163	156	149	143
22	193	184	175	167	160	153	146
23	199	189	180	172	164	156	150
24	205	195	185	176	168	160	152
25	211	200	189	180	171	163	155
26	216	205	194	184	174	166	158
27	222	209	198	187	178	169	160
28	227	214	202	191	181	171	163
29	232	218	206	194	184	174	165
30	237	223	209	197	186	176	167

Time on Your Side

You may need less money than you think to provide for your future—depending on how far off the future is in your plans. For instance, if you'll need $10,000 ten years from now, $6,100 left in the bank at 5 percent interest will become $10,000 with no further saving. If you can wait twenty years you'll need only $3,800 now. The chart below can be used to show how much you need now to provide for the future. *Example One:* To provide $15,000 for a college education twelve years from now, a fund of $8,400 left at 5 percent interest during that time will grow to the sum needed. Read down the chart to the proper line (in this case twelve years in the future), and across to the designated interest factor (5 percent in the example) and you find the factor .56 which is then multiplied by $15,000 to show the amount needed now. *Example Two:* If you have a fund now and want to find what it will become in the future if left at interest, simply pick a year in the future and an interest factor as before, but then *divide* by the number you find in the table. Thus a $5,000 life insurance death benefit left at 5 percent interest for twenty-five years will become $16,666.

Years before Income Is Needed	3%	3½ %	4%	Discount Factors 4½ %	5%	5½ %	6%
1	.97	.97	.96	.96	.95	.95	.94
2	.94	.93	.92	.92	.91	.90	.89
3	.92	.90	.89	.88	.86	.85	.84

(Table cont'd.)

Years before Income Is Needed	3%	3½ %	4%	4½ %	5%	5½ %	6%
				Discount Factors			
4	.89	.87	.85	.84	.82	.81	.79
5	.86	.84	.82	.80	.78	.77	.75
6	.84	.81	.79	.77	.75	.73	.70
7	.81	.79	.76	.73	.71	.69	.67
8	.79	.76	.73	.70	.68	.65	.63
9	.77	.73	.70	.67	.64	.62	.59
10	.74	.71	.68	.64	.61	.59	.56
11	.72	.68	.65	.62	.58	.55	.53
12	.70	.66	.62	.59	.56	.53	.50
13	.68	.64	.60	.56	.53	.50	.47
14	.66	.62	.58	.54	.51	.47	.44
15	.64	.60	.56	.52	.48	.45	.42
16	.62	.58	.53	.49	.46	.42	.39
17	.61	.56	.51	.47	.44	.40	.37
18	.59	.54	.49	.45	.42	.38	.35
19	.57	.52	.47	.43	.40	.36	.33
20	.55	.50	.46	.41	.38	.34	.31
21	.54	.49	.44	.40	.36	.32	.29
22	.52	.47	.42	.38	.34	.31	.28
23	.51	.45	.41	.36	.33	.29	.26
24	.49	.44	.39	.35	.31	.28	.25
25	.48	.42	.38	.33	.30	.26	.23
26	.46	.41	.36	.32	.28	.25	.22
27	.45	.40	.35	.30	.27	.24	.21
28	.44	.38	.33	.29	.26	.22	.20
29	.42	.37	.32	.28	.24	.21	.18
30	.41	.36	.31	.27	.23	.20	.17
31	.40	.34	.30	.26	.22	.19	.16
32	.39	.33	.29	.24	.21	.18	.15
33	.38	.32	.27	.23	.20	.17	.15
34	.37	.31	.26	.22	.19	.16	.14
35	.36	.30	.25	.21	.18	.15	.13
36	.35	.29	.24	.21	.17	.15	.12
37	.33	.28	.23	.20	.16	.14	.12
38	.33	.27	.23	.19	.16	.13	.11
39	.32	.26	.22	.18	.15	.12	.10
40	.31	.25	.21	.17	.14	.12	.10
41	.30	.24	.20	.16	.14	.11	.09
42	.29	.24	.19	.16	.13	.11	.09
43	.28	.23	.19	.15	.12	.10	.08
44	.27	.22	.18	.14	.12	.09	.08
45	.26	.21	.17	.14	.11	.09	.07

APPENDIX C
The Best's Ratings

Each year an independent life insurance publication called *Best's Life Insurance Reports* issues ratings for the more than 1,400 insurance companies doing business in the United States. Simply stated, "Best's rating" is a measure of a life insurance company's financial stability. The highest rating Best issues is "most substantial." In 1974 (the latest completed survey year), 141 life insurance companies earned the "most substantial" rating. The companies are listed below in alphabetical order along with the mailing address of each company's home office.

These ratings are financial indicators only; they are intended to measure a company's ability to keep its contractual word rather than to show its attitude toward its policyholders—also an important consideration in choosing an insurance company. Remember that Best also rates some perfectly sound life insurance companies "substantial" or "very substantial," so that not being on this list does not automatically mean an insurer is critically weak. If the insurance company you are considering, or are currently insured by, is not on this list you owe it to yourself to find out why.

Acacia Mutual Life Insurance Company
51 Louisiana Ave. N.W.
Washington, D.C. 20001

Aetna Life Insurance Company
151 Farmington Ave.
Hartford, Conn. 06115

Aid Association for Lutherans
222 West College Ave.
Appleton, Wis. 54911

Allstate Life Insurance Company
Allstate Plaza
Northbrook, Ill. 60062

American General Life Insurance Company
P. O. Box 1931
Houston, Tex. 77001

American General Life Insurance Company of Delaware
P. O. Box 1526
Houston, Tex. 77001

American Mutual Life Insurance Company
Liberty Building
Des Moines, Iowa 50307

American National Insurance Company
One Moody Plaza
Galveston, Tex. 77550

American United Life Insurance Company
P. O. Box 368
Indianapolis, Ind. 46208

Bankers Life Company
711 High St.
Des Moines, Iowa 50307

Bankers National Life Insurance Company
P. O. Box 500
Parsippany, N.J. 07054

Beneficial Life Insurance Company
57 West South Temple St.
Salt Lake City, Utah 84101

Berkshire Life Insurance Company
700 South St.
Pittsfield, Mass. 01201

Business Men's Assurance Company of America
BMA Tower
Penn Valley Park
Kansas City, Mo. 64141

California-Western States Life Insurance Company
P. O. Box 959
Sacramento, Cal. 95804

Canada Life Assurance Company
330 University Ave.
Toronto, Ontario, MG5 1R7, Canada

Central Life Assurance Company
P. O. Box 1555
Des Moines, Iowa 50306

Columbus Mutual Life Insurance Company
303 E. Broad St.
Columbus, Ohio 43215

Commonwealth Life Insurance Company
Broadway at 4th St.
Louisville, Ky. 40202

Confederation Life Insurance Company
321 Bloor St. E.
Toronto, Ontario, M4W 169, Canada

Connecticut General Life Insurance Company
Hartford, Conn. 06115

Connecticut Mutual Life Insurance Company
140 Garden St.
Hartford, Conn. 06115

Continental American Life Insurance Company
11th & Kings St.
Wilmington, Del. 19899

Country Life Insurance Company
1701 Towanda Ave.
Bloomington, Ill. 61301

Crown Life Insurance Company
120 Bloor St. E.
Toronto, Ontario, M4W 188, Canada

Dominion Life Assurance Company
111 Westmouth Rd.
Waterloo, Ontario, N2L 2L6, Canada

Durham Life Insurance Company
P. O. Box 27807
Raleigh, N.C. 27611

Equitable Life Assurance Society of the United States
1285 Avenue of the Americas
New York, N.Y. 10019

Equitable Life Insurance Company
3900 Wisconsin Ave.
Washington, D.C. 20016

Equitable Life Insurance Company of Iowa
604 Locust St.
Des Moines, Iowa 50306

Farm Bureau Life Insurance Company
10th and Grand Ave.
Des Moines, Iowa 50307

Fidelity Mutual Life Insurance Company
Philadelphia, Pa. 19101

Fidelity Union Life Insurance Company
P. O. Box 2580
Dallas, Tex. 75221

Franklin Life Insurance Company
Springfield, Ill. 62713

General American Life Insurance Company
15th and Locust Sts.
St. Louis, Mo. 63166

Government Employees Life Insurance Company
1705 L St. N.W.
Washington, D.C. 20036

Great Southern Life Insurance Company
3121 Buffalo Speedway
Houston, Tex. 77006

The Great-West Life Assurance Company
60 Osborne St. N.
Winnipeg, Manitoba, R3C 1V3, Canada

Guarantee Mutual Life Company of America
8721 Indian Hills Dr.
Omaha, Neb. 68114

Guardian Life Insurance Company of America
201 Park Ave. S.
New York, N.Y. 10003

Hartford Life Insurance Company
Hartford Plaza
Hartford, Conn. 06115

Home Beneficial Life Insurance Company
3901 W. Broad St.
Richmond, Va. 23230

Home Life Insurance Company
253 Broadway
New York, N.Y. 10007

I.D.S. Life Insurance Co. of Minnesota
I.D.S. Tower
Minneapolis, Minn. 55402

Imperial Life Assurance Company of Canada
95 St. Clair Ave. W.
Toronto, Ontario, M4V 1N7, Canada

Indianapolis Life Insurance Company
2960 N. Meridian St.
Indianapolis, Ind. 46208

Integon Life Insurance Corporation
420 N. Spruce St.
Winston-Salem, N.C. 27102

Interstate Life & Accident Insurance Company
540 McCallie Ave.
Chattanooga, Tenn. 37402

Jefferson Standard Life Insurance Company
Jefferson Square
Greensboro, N.C. 27420

John Hancock Mutual Life Insurance Company
200 Berkeley St.
Boston, Mass. 02117

Kansas City Life Insurance Company
3520 Broadway
Kansas City, Mo. 64111

Kansas Farm Life Insurance Company
2321 Anderson Ave.
Manhattan, Kan. 66502

Knights of Columbus
One Columbus Plaza
New Haven, Conn. 06507

Lafayette Life Insurance Company
2203 S. 18th St.
Lafayette, Ind. 47902

Lamar Life Insurance Company
P. O. Box 880
Jackson, Miss. 39205

Liberty Life Insurance Company
Wade Hampton Blvd.
Greenville, S.C. 29607

Liberty National Life Insurance Company
P. O. Box 2612
Birmingham, Ala. 35202

Life and Casualty Insurance Company of Tennessee
Life and Casualty Tower
Nashville, Tenn. 37219

Life Insurance Company of Georgia
Life of Georgia Tower
Atlanta, Ga. 30308

Life Insurance Company of Virginia
Capitol and 10th Sts.
Richmond, Va. 23219

Lincoln National Life Insurance Company
1301 S. Harrison St.
Fort Wayne, Ind. 46801

Loyal Protective Life Insurance Company
11 Deerfield St.
Boston, Mass. 00217

Lutheran Brotherhood
701 2nd Avenue South
Minneapolis, Minn. 55402

Lutheran Mutual Life Insurance Company
201-211 1st St. S.E.
Waverly, Iowa 50677

Manufacturers Life Insurance Company
200 Bloor St. E.
Toronto, Ontario, M4W E4, Canada

Massachusetts Mutual Life Insurance Company
1925 State St.
Springfield, Mass. 01111

Metropolitan Life Insurance Company
1 Madison Ave.
New York, N.Y. 10010

Midland Mutual Life Insurance Company
250 E. Broad St.
Columbus, Ohio 43215

Midwestern United Life Insurance Company
7551 U.S. Highway 24 W.
Fort Wayne, Ind. 46804

Minnesota Mutual Life Insurance Company
345 Cedar St.
St. Paul, Minn. 55101

Monarch Life Insurance Company
1250 State St.
Springfield, Mass. 01101

Monumental Life Insurance Company
Charles & Chase Sts.
Baltimore, Md. 21202

Mutual Benefit Life Insurance Company
520 Broad St.
Newark, N.J. 07101

Mutual Life Insurance Company of New York
1740 Broadway
New York, N.Y. 10019

Mutual Trust Life Insurance Company
77 S. Wacker Dr.
Chicago, Ill. 60606

National Fidelity Life Insurance Company
1002 Walnut St.
Kansas City, Mo. 64106

National Guardian Life Insurance Company
2 E. Gilman St.
Madison, Wis. 53704

National Life & Accident Insurance Company
National Life Center
Nashville, Tenn. 37250

National Life Insurance Company
National Life Drive
Montpelier, Vt. 05602

National Life Insurance Company
246 N. High St.
Columbus, Ohio 43216

National Travelers Life
820 Keosauqua Way
Des Plaines, Iowa 50308

New England Mutual Life Insurance Company
501 Boylston St.
Boston, Mass. 02117

New York Life Insurance Company
51 Madison Ave.
New York, N.Y. 10010

North American Company for Life and Health Insurance
P. O. Box 466
Chicago, Ill. 60690

North American Life Assurance Company
105 Adelaide St. W.
Toronto, Ontario, M5H 1P9, Canada

North American Reassurance Company
245 Park Ave.
New York, N.Y. 10017

Northern Life Insurance Company
110 3rd Ave.
Seattle, Wash. 98104

Northwestern Mutual Life Insurance Company
720 E. Wisconsin Ave.
Milwaukee, Wis. 53202

Northwestern National Life Insurance Company
20 Washington Ave. S.
Minneapolis, Minn. 55440

Occidental Life Insurance Company of California
P. O. Box 2101
Terminal Annex
Los Angeles, Cal. 90051

Ohio National Life Insurance Company
William Howard Taft Road at Highland Ave.
Cincinnati, Ohio 45219

Ohio State Life Insurance Company
100 E. Broad St.
Columbus, Ohio 43215

Pacific Mutual Life Insurance Company
700 Newport Center Dr.
Newport Beach, Cal. 92663

Pan-American Life Insurance Company
P. O. Box 60219
New Orleans, La. 70160

Paul Revere Life Insurance Company
18 Chestnut St.
Worcester, Mass. 01680

Penn Mutual Life Insurance Company
Independence Square
Philadelphia, Pa. 19172

Philadelphia Life Insurance Company
111-115 N. Broad St.
Philadelphia, Pa. 19107

Phoenix Mutual Life Insurance Company
One American Row
Hartford, Conn. 06115

Pilot Life Insurance Company
P. O. Box 20727
Greensboro, N.C. 27420

Presbyterian Ministers' Fund
1809 Walnut St.
Philadelphia, Pa. 19103

Protective Life Insurance Company
2027-29 1st Ave. N.
Birmingham, Ala. 35203

Provident Life and Accident Insurance Company
Fountain Square
Chattanooga, Tenn. 37402

Provident Mutual Life Insurance Company of Philadelphia
4601 Market St.
Philadelphia, Pa. 19101

Prudential Insurance Company of America
Prudential Plaza
Newark, N.J. 07101

Reliance Standard Life Insurance Company (Chicago)
4 Penn Center Plaza
Philadelphia, Pa. 19103

SAFECO Life Insurance Company
SAFECO Plaza
Seattle, Wash. 98185

Security Life and Accident Company
Security Life Building
Denver, Colo. 80802

Security Mutual Life Insurance Company of New York
Court House Square
Binghamton, N.Y. 13902

Shenandoah Life Insurance Company
P. O. Box 2421
Roanoke, Va. 24010

Southern Farm Bureau Life Insurance Company
P. O. Box 78
Jackson, Miss. 39205

Southland Life Insurance Company
Southland Center
Dallas, Tex. 75201

Southwestern Life Insurance Company
P. O. Box 2699
Dallas, Tex. 75221

Standard Insurance Company
P. O. Box 71
Portland, Ore. 97207

State Farm Life and Accident Assurance Company
112 E. Washington St.
Bloomington, Ill. 60701

State Farm Life Insurance Company
State Farm Insurance Building
Bloomington, Ill. 61701

State Mutual Life Assurance of America
440 Lincoln St.
Worcester, Mass. 01605

Sun Life Assurance Company of Canada
P. O. Box 6075
Montreal, Quebec, H3C 3G5, Canada

Sun Life Insurance Company of America
Sun Life Building
Charles Center
Baltimore, Md. 21201

Sunset Life Insurance Company of America
3200 Capitol Blvd.
Olympia, Wash. 98507

Teachers Insurance and Annuity Association of America
730 3rd Ave.
New York, N.Y. 10017

Texas Life Insurance Company
P. O. Box 830
Waco, Tex. 76703

Travelers Insurance Company
One Tower Square
Hartford, Conn. 06115

Union Central Life Insurance Company
P. O. Box 179
Cincinnati, Ohio 45201

Union National Life Insurance Company
P. O. Box 2348
Baton Rouge, La. 70821

United American Insurance Company
P. O. Box 810
Dallas, Tex. 75221

United Benefit Life Insurance Company
Dodge at 33rd St.
Omaha, Neb. 68131

United Farm Bureau Family Life Insurance Company
130 E. Washington St.
Indianapolis, Ind. 46204

United Fidelity Life Insurance Company
1025 Elm St.
Dallas, Tex. 75202

United States Life Insurance Company
1701 Pennsylvania Ave. N.W.
Washington, D.C. 20006

United States Life Insurance Company in the City of New York
125 Maiden Lane
New York, N.Y. 10038

Volunteer State Life Insurance Company
The Volunteer State Life Building
Chattanooga, Tenn. 37402

Washington National Insurance Company
1630 Chicago Ave.
Evanston, Ill. 60621

Western Life Insurance Company
385 Washington St.
St. Paul, Minn. 55102

Western and Southern Life Insurance Company
400 Broadway
Cincinnati, Ohio 45202

Wisconsin National Life Insurance Company
P. O. Box 740
Oshkosh, Wis. 54901

APPENDIX D

Some Key Factors in the Search for Straight Life Insurance

Of all the insurance purchases one is likely to make straight life insurance can be the most difficult to evaluate. Even the choice between a participating policy (one in which a policyholder has a share in the company which entitles him to dividends in addition to normal cash accumulation) or nonparticipating (where no dividend is given) can be tricky. While the so-called "non-par" policy usually costs less, it also pays less in cash value. On the other hand, the increased cash value of participating straight life insurance is not guaranteed (though many insurance companies exist that have never missed a dividend payment).

The following charts have been set up to compare the costs of straight life insurance by the largest companies (as indexed by volume of business done in the state of Pennsylvania during the years 1972, 1973, and 1974) for both participating and nonparticipating policies. A typical entry will look like this:

	Annual Premium	Cash Value 10/20 Year	Cost Index 10/20 Year
Mutual Benefit Life Ins. Co.	$153	$ 992	$4.02
		2,260	3.02

In this example (for $10,000 participating straight life coverage purchased at age twenty), the entry means that the Mutual Benefit Life Insurance Company offers the policy for $153 per year and that at the end of ten years the policy would contain $992 in cash value, which would grow to $2,260 at the end of twenty years. The cost index is a method of computing the true cost of owning the policy by comparing premium paid with cash value assuming a 4 percent interest rate. In this case, the 4.02 cost index for ten years means that the Mutual Benefit policy costs 30 percent less than a policy rated at, say, 5.75.

Keep in mind that all entries in the charts should be used in evaluating a particular policy. For example, where one company seems to offer much more cash value than another for the same premium paid, look at the cost index. If the cost index is nearly the same for both, you can assume that the company with the lower cash value figure is making up the difference by paying higher dividends or paying them earlier in the life of the policy.

The following reference numbers appear in the charts:

1. The policy includes waiver of premium for disability at no extra premium, but the cost factor has been adjusted to consider this.
2. Policy is issued on a "last birthday" basis instead of "nearest birthday."
3. The policy is a modified premium contract—meaning that the premiums are lower during the early years. The cost factor is adjusted to consider this.
4. The premiums for females are generally lower.
5. The figures shown are valid only for policies at standard rates.
6. The interest-adjusted surrender cost, per $1,000 of face amount, using a 4 percent interest factor.
7. Ranked according to the average cost index averaged between ten and twenty years.

NOTE: The following material on straight life policies as well as that in the appendix that follows (on term life policies) has been developed from "A Shopper's Guide to Straight Life Insurance" and "A Shopper's Guide to Term Life Insurance." Both booklets are available at $1 each by writing: Consumer Insurance, 813 National Press Building, Washington, D.C. 20004.

MALE AGE 20 [4]—DATA FOR PARTICIPATING POLICIES
SOLD BY THE 35 LARGEST COMPANIES [5]
$10,000 STRAIGHT LIFE POLICY

Company [7]	Annual Premium	Cash Value 10/20 Year	Cost Index 10/20 Year [6]
1. Connecticut Mutual Life Insurance Co.	$135	$ 937	$2.82
		2,161	2.11
2. Provident Mutual Life Insurance Co. of Philadelphia [3]	132	920	3.24
		2,150	2.68
3. The Northwestern Mutual Life Insurance Co.	157	1,086	3.51
		2,518	2.58
4. Bankers Life Co. (Iowa) [2]	117	800	3.86
		2,190	2.64
5. Massachusetts Mutual Life Insurance Co.[3]	145	982	3.91
		2,425	2.83
6. Home Life Insurance Co. (N.Y.) [3]	147	720	4.72
		2,110	2.31
7. Mutual Benefit Life Insurance Co.	153	992	4.02
		2,260	3.02
8. Phoenix Mutual Life Insurance Co.	157	1,130	4.54
		2,710	2.57
9. The Guardian Life Insurance Co. of America	135	983	4.28
		2,472	2.95
10. National Life Insurance Co. (Vt.)	149	1,040	4.34
		2,478	2.91
11. New York Life Insurance Co. [3]	150	900	4.21
		2,130	3.23
12. Sun Life Assurance Co. of Canada	153	876	4.55
		2,322	2.91
13. The Canada Life Assurance Co.	141	980	4.23
		2,360	3.27
14. Connecticut General Life Insurance Co.	139	1,100	3.96
		2,500	3.95
15. The Great-West Life Assurance Co.	150	990	4.40
		2,360	3.53
16. The Penn Mutual Life Insurance Co.[3]	115	760	4.50
		2,090	3.51

Company [7]	Annual Premium	Cash Value 10/20 Year	Cost Index 10/20 Year [6]
17. New England Mutual Life Insurance Co.	155	965 2,364	4.98 3.17
18. Nationwide Life Insurance Co.[2]	151	956 2,386	4.61 3.59
19. State Mutual Life Assurance Co. of America (Mass.)	142	937 2,161	4.86 3.41
20. The Prudential Insurance Co. of America [1, 2, 3]	156	1,020 2,350	4.65 3.71
21. Crown Life Insurance Co.[2]	120	720 2,000	5.00 3.56
22. State Farm Life Insurance Co.[1, 2]	146	852 2,187	5.33 3.31
23. Franklin Life Insurance Co.	146	875 2,322	5.23 3.43
24. The Western & Southern Life Insurance Co.[1, 2, 3]	151	730 2,190	4.60 4.33
25. The Manufacturers Life Insurance Co.	128	670 1,940	5.48 3.47
26. The Equitable Life Assurance Society of the U.S. (N.Y.)	152	880 2,170	5.35 3.69
27. Republic National Life Insurance Co.	139	880 2,320	5.07 4.06
28. Metropolitan Life Insurance Co.[1, 2]	152	1,010 2,460	5.48 3.66
29. The Mutual Life Insurance Co. of New York [1]	152	1,000 2,370	5.46 3.71
30. Occidental Life Insurance Co. of California	154	990 2,750	5.75 3.43
31. The Lincoln National Life Insurance Co.	155	931 2,350	5.72 3.46
32. John Hancock Mutual Life Insurance Co.[3]	150	800 2,200	5.45 4.19
33. Continental Assurance Co.	158	940 2,590	6.09 3.62
34. American National Insurance Co.[1, 2]	158	880 2,400	6.14 4.15
35. Aetna Life Insurance Co.	166	870 2,390	8.51 4.72

MALE AGE 20 [4]—DATA FOR PARTICIPATING POLICIES
SOLD BY THE 35 LARGEST COMPANIES [5]
$25,000 STRAIGHT LIFE POLICY

Company [7]	Annual Premium	Cash Value 10/20 Year	Cost Index 10/20 Year [6]
1. Connecticut Mutual Life Insurance Co.	$325	$2,342 5,403	$2.32 1.61
2. Provident Mutual Life Insurance Co. of Philadelphia [3]	318	2,300 5,375	2.76 2.20
3. Massachusetts Mutual Life Insurance Co.	353	2,601 6,195	3.22 2.09
4. The Northwestern Mutual Life Insurance Co.	384	2,716 6,294	3.15 2.22
5. Bankers Life Co. (Iowa) [2]	280	2,000 5,475	3.38 2.16
6. Home Life Insurance Co. (N.Y.) [3]	354	1,900 5,275	3.89 1.81
7. Sun Life Assurance Co. of Canada	377	2,625 5,910	3.04 2.69
8. Mutual Benefit Life Insurance Co.	366	2,480 5,650	3.37 2.37
9. The Guardian Life Insurance Co. of America	320	2,458 6,179	3.56 2.23
10. The Equitable Life Assurance Society of U.S. (N.Y.)	360	2,350 5,425	3.52 2.51
11. The Penn Mutual Insurance Co.	354	2,625 6,225	3.84 2.23
12. Nationwide Life Insurance Co.[2]	350	2,654 5,967	3.11 3.00
13. Phoenix Mutual Life Insurance Co.	380	2,825 6,775	4.06 2.09
14. New York Life Insurance Co.[3]	363	2,250 5,325	3.71 2.73
15. National Life Insurance Co. (Vt.)	364	2,601 6,195	4.02 2.59
16. State Mutual Life Assurance Co. of America (Mass.)	335	2,342 5,403	4.06 2.61
17. Continental Assurance Co.[3]	366	2,500 6,400	4.19 2.50
18. The Great-West Life Assurance Co.	315	1,975 5,400	4.11 2.65
19. The Lincoln National Life Insurance Co.	383	2,611 5,877	4.18 2.63

Company [7]	Annual Premium	Cash Value 10/20 Year	Cost Index 10/20 Year [6]
20. New England Mutual Life Insurance Co.	380	2,625 5,909	3.99 2.87
21. Mutual Life Insurance Co. of New York [1]	369	2,650 5,925	4.16 2.86
22. John Hancock Mutual Life Insurance Co. [3]	344	2,000 5,500	4.25 2.99
23. The Prudential Insurance Co. of America [1, 2]	367	2,675 5,975	4.12 3.14
24. Crown Life Insurance Co. [2]	284	1,800 5,000	4.40 2.96
25. Occidental Life Insurance Co. of California	362	2,475 6,875	4.85 2.53
26. State Farm Life Insurance Co. [1, 2]	350	2,130 5,468	4.73 2.71
27. Connecticut General Life Insurance Co.	344	2,750 6,250	3.76 3.75
28. The Canada Life Assurance Co.	326	1,750 4,925	5.02 2.79
29. Republic National Life Insurance Co.	370	1,925 6,110	5.41 2.41
30. The Manufacturers Life Insurance Co.	306	1,675 4,850	4.94 2.93
31. Franklin Life Insurance Co.	356	2,188 5,804	4.87 3.07
32. Metropolitan Life Insurance Co. [1, 2]	382	2,525 6,150	4.88 3.06
33. The Western & Southern Life Insurance Co. [1, 2, 3]	367	1,825 5,475	4.27 3.96
34. American National Insurance Co. [1, 2]	378	2,200 6,000	5.42 3.43
35. Aetna Life Insurance Co.	402	2,575 5,975	5.88 3.58

MALE AGE 35 [4]—DATA FOR PARTICIPATING POLICIES
SOLD BY THE 35 LARGEST COMPANIES [5]
$10,000 STRAIGHT LIFE POLICY

Company [7]	Annual Premium	Cash Value 10/20 Year	Cost Index 10/20 Year [6]
1. The Northwestern Mutual Life Insurance Co.	$235	$1,732 3,751	$4.65 4.13
2. Connecticut Mutual Life Insurance Co.	218	1,600 3,421	4.74 4.45
3. Bankers Life Co. (Iowa) [2]	188	1,430 3,440	4.98 4.40
4. Massachusetts Mutual Life Insurance Co.[3]	222	1,600 3,676	5.11 4.63
5. Provident Mutual Life Insurance Co. of Philadelphia [3]	210	1,570 3,400	4.94 4.94
6. Home Life Insurance Co. (N.Y.) [3]	220	1,200 3,210	6.03 4.31
7. National Life Insurance Co. (Vt.)	228	1,687 3,749	6.01 4.64
8. Mutual Benefit Life Insurance Co.	230	1,656 3,510	5.59 5.09
9. Phoenix Mutual Life Insurance Co.	234	1,760 3,930	6.07 4.64
10. The Canada Life Assurance Co.	214	1,610 3,570	5.67 5.30
11. New York Life Insurance Co. [3]	231	1,540 3,380	5.93 5.23
12. Sun Life Assurance Co. of Canada	234	1,495 3,525	6.16 5.01
13. The Guardian Life Insurance Co. of America	210	1,585 3,726	6.27 5.10
14. The Great-West Life Assurance Co.	229	1,640 3,570	5.80 5.58
15. New England Mutual Life Insurance Co.	232	1,638 3,602	6.34 5.05
16. Nationwide Life Insurance Co.[2]	235	1,601 3,613	6.20 5.47
17. State Mutual Life Assurance Co. of America (Mass.)	220	1,600 3,421	6.32 5.35
18. The Penn Mutual Life Insurance Co.[3]	202	1,350 3,310	6.06 5.75
19. Crown Life Insurance Co.[2]	189	1,330 3,210	6.39 5.46

Company [7]	Annual Premium	Cash Value 10/20 Year	Cost Index 10/20 Year [6]
20. The Manufacturers Life Insurance Co.	197	1,280 3,170	6.82 5.18
21. State Farm Life Insurance Co.[1,2]	227	1,487 3,437	6.91 5.28
22. Occidental Life Insurance Co. of California	229	1,610 3,980	7.28 5.22
23. The Lincoln National Life Insurance Co.	236	1,581 3,569	7.10 5.57
24. The Prudential Insurance Co. of America [1,2,3]	243	1,660 3,570	6.90 6.22
25. The Equitable Life Assurance Society of U.S. (N.Y.)	230	1,530 3,430	7.20 5.97
26. The Western & Southern Life Insurance Co.[1,2,3]	236	1,250 3,340	6.27 6.96
27. Franklin Life Insurance Co.	226	1,496 3,525	7.41 5.90
28. The Mutual Life Insurance Co. of New York [1]	234	1,660 3,610	7.36 6.03
29. Connecticut General Life Insurance Co.	220	1,740 3,720	6.35 7.07
30. Continental Assurance Co.	239	1,550 3,830	8.13 5.62
31. John Hancock Mutual Life Insurance Co.[3]	231	1,320 3,370	7.52 6.57
32. Metropolitan Life Insurance Co.[1,2]	248	1,660 3,700	7.89 6.24
33. American National Insurance Co.[1,2]	242	1,530 3,650	8.43 6.22
34. Republic National Life Insurance Co.	222	1,500 3,530	7.91 7.57
35. Aetna Life Insurance Co.	244	1,510 3,610	10.61 6.51

MALE AGE 35 [4]—DATA FOR PARTICIPATING POLICIES
SOLD BY THE 35 LARGEST COMPANIES [5]
$25,000 STRAIGHT LIFE POLICY

Company [7]	Annual Premium	Cash Value 10/20 Year	Cost Index 10/20 Year [6]
1. Massachusetts Mutual Life Insurance Co.	$545	$4,218 9,373	$3.97 3.60
2. The Northwestern Mutual Life Insurance Co.	578	4,331 9,378	4.29 3.77
3. Connecticut Mutual Life Insurance Co.	534	3,999 8,552	4.24 3.95
4. Bankers Life Co. (Iowa) [2]	459	3,575 8,600	4.50 3.92
5. Provident Mutual Life Insurance Co. of Philadelphia [3]	512	3,925 8,500	4.46 4.46
6. Home Life Insurance Co. (N.Y.) [3]	538	3,100 8,025	5.21 3.81
7. Sun Life Assurance Co. of Canada	579	4,289 9,007	4.33 4.74
8. Mutual Benefit Life Insurance Co.	559	4,141 8,774	4.94 4.44
9. Nationwide Life Insurance Co. [2]	563	4,313 9,034	4.52 4.86
10. The Penn Mutual Life Insurance Co.	537	4,250 9,400	5.42 4.02
11. The Equitable Life Assurance Society of U.S. (N.Y.)	556	4,000 8,575	5.03 4.55
12. Phoenix Mutual Life Insurance Co.	572	4,400 9,825	5.59 4.16
13. The Guardian Life Insurance Co. of America	508	3,963 9,315	5.55 4.38
14. National Life Insurance Co. (Vt.)	561	4,218 9,373	5.69 4.32
15. State Mutual Life Assurance Co. of America (Mass.)	530	3,999 8,552	5.52 4.55
16. New York Life Insurance Co. [3]	564	3,850 8,450	5.43 4.73
17. New England Mutual Life Insurance Co.	574	4,288 9,004	5.42 4.75
18. The Great-West Life Assurance Co.	501	3,550 8,500	5.63 4.68
19. Continental Assurance Co. [3]	570	4,100 9,500	6.00 4.50

Company [7]	Annual Premium	Cash Value 10/20 Year	Cost Index 10/20 Year [6]
20. The Canada Life Assurance Co.	504	3,350 8,075	6.10 4.42
21. Crown Life Insurance Co.[2]	458	3,325 8,025	5.79 4.86
22. Occidental Life Insurance Co. of California	551	4,025 9,950	6.38 4.32
23. Mutual Life Insurance Co. of New York [1]	574	4,300 9,025	5.89 4.83
24. The Lincoln National Life Insurance Co.	590	4,251 8,926	5.97 4.87
25. The Manufacturers Life Insurance Co.	479	3,200 7,925	6.28 4.64
26. State Farm Life Insurance Co.[1,2]	554	3,718 8,593	6.31 4.68
27. Republic National Life Insurance Co.	574	3,475 9,225	6.88 4.26
28. John Hancock Mutual Life Insurance Co.[3]	548	3,300 8,425	6.32 5.37
29. The Prudential Insurance Co. of America [1,2]	580	4,325 9,075	6.45 5.63
30. The Western & Southern Life Insurance Co.[1,2,3]	580	3,125 8,350	5.94 6.58
31. Franklin Life Insurance Co.	557	3,740 8,814	7.05 5.54
32. Metropolitan Life Insurance Co.[1,2]	605	4,150 9,250	7.29 5.64
33. Connecticut General Life Insurance Co.	546	4,350 9,300	6.15 6.87
34. American National Insurance Co.[1,2]	588	3,825 9,125	7.70 5.50
35. Aetna Life Insurance Co.	606	4,175 9,025	8.01 5.43

MALE AGE 50 [4]—DATA FOR PARTICIPATING POLICIES
SOLD BY THE 35 LARGEST COMPANIES [5]
$10,000 STRAIGHT LIFE POLICY

Company [7]	Annual Premium	Cash Value 10/20 Year	Cost Index 10/20 Year [6]
1. The Northwestern Mutual Life Insurance Co.	$405	$2,597 5,178	$11.39 12.29
2. Phoenix Mutual Life Insurance Co.	392	2,560 5,220	12.02 12.12
3. New York Life Insurance Co.[3]	399	2,390 4,800	11.57 12.80
4. Bankers Life Co. (Iowa) [2]	339	2,270 4,830	11.70 12.91
5. Massachusetts Mutual Life Insurance Co.[3]	387	2,382 5,038	12.01 12.83
6. Provident Mutual Life Insurance Co. of Phildelphia [3]	380	2,440 4,830	11.76 13.30
7. Connecticut Mutual Life Insurance Co.	398	2,491 4,863	12.22 12.93
8. Home Life Insurance Co. (N.Y.) [3]	387	1,670 4,350	13.23 12.59
9. New England Mutual Life Insurance Co.	399	2,528 4,997	12.88 12.97
10. National Life Insurance Co. (Vt.)	388	2,526 5,142	13.49 12.51
11. Mutual Benefit Life Insurance Co.	398	2,541 4,929	12.70 13.67
12. Nationwide Life Insurance Co.[2]	410	2,411 4,952	13.17 14.20
13. Sun Life Assurance Co. of Canada	409	2,278 4,854	13.72 13.79
14. The Prudential Insurance Co. of America [1, 2, 3]	435	2,470 4,880	13.81 13.75
15. The Manufacturers Life Insurance Co.	344	2,080 4,590	14.04 13.60
16. The Great-West Life Assurance Co.	400	2,480 4,920	13.29 14.46
17. State Mutual Life Assurance Co. of America (Mass.)	391	2,491 4,863	13.95 13.83
18. Crown Life Insurance Co.[2]	348	2,130 4,570	13.70 14.24
19. The Penn Mutual Life Insurance Co.[3]	392	2,130 4,690	13.65 14.76

Company [7]	Annual Premium	Cash Value 10/20 Year	Cost Index 10/20 Year [6]
20. The Canada Life Assurance Co.	385	2,410 4,920	13.75 14.74
21. The Guardian Life Insurance Co.	362	2,343 5,072	14.50 14.06
22. The Mutual Life Insurance Co. of New York [1]	416	2,540 5,000	14.59 14.46
23. State Farm Life Insurance Co. [1, 2]	409	2,295 4,826	14.98 14.37
24. Occidental Life Insurance Co. of California	394	2,370 5,260	15.45 14.33
25. John Hancock Mutual Life Insurance Co. [3]	408	1,910 4,620	15.02 14.90
26. The Equitable Life Assurance Society of U.S. (N.Y.)	401	2,400 4,870	15.21 14.81
27. The Lincoln National Life Insurance Co.	409	2,407 4,915	15.22 14.83
28. Franklin Life Insurance Co.	400	2,276 4,854	15.58 15.00
29. Continental Assurance Co.	404	2,300 5,150	16.93 14.45
30. Connecticut General Life Insurance Co.	394	2,560 5,060	14.58 17.03
31. American National Insurance Co. [1, 2]	426	2,360 5,040	16.72 15.35
32. Metropolitan Life Insurance Co. [1, 2]	427	2,490 5,080	16.83 15.33
33. Aetna Life Insurance Co.	414	2,330 4,940	18.34 13.85
34. The Western & Southern Life Insurance Co. [1, 2, 3]	414	1,830 4,590	14.96 17.89
35. Republic National Life Insurance Co.	402	2,300 4,890	17.79 18.87

MALE AGE 50 [4]—DATA FOR PARTICIPATING POLICIES
SOLD BY THE 35 LARGEST COMPANIES [5]
$25,000 STRAIGHT LIFE POLICY

Company [7]	Annual Premium	Cash Value 10/20 Year	Cost Index 10/20 Year [6]
1. Massachusetts Mutual Life Insurance Co.	$ 957	$ 6,314 12,854	$11.04 11.77
2. The Northwestern Mutual Life Insurance Co.	1,004	6,492 12,946	11.03 11.93
3. Phoenix Mutual Life Insurance Co.	969	6,400 13,050	11.54 11.64
4. New York Life Insurance Co. [3]	984	5,975 12,000	11.07 12.30
5. Bankers Life Co. (Iowa) [2]	834	5,675 12,075	11.22 12.43
6. Provident Mutual Life Insurance Co. of Philadelphia [3]	937	6,100 12,075	11.28 12.82
7. Connecticut Mutual Life Insurance Co.	982	6,227 12,158	11.72 12.43
8. Home Life Insurance Co. (N.Y.) [3]	954	4,325 10,875	12.25 12.09
9. Sun Life Assurance Co. of Canada	1,017	6,488 12,504	11.23 13.42
10. The Penn Mutual Life Insurance Co.	954	6,350 12,975	12.69 11.96
11. Nationwide Life Insurance Co. [2]	1,002	6,456 12,393	11.11 13.58
12. New England Mutual Life Insurance Co.	990	6,484 12,494	12.05 12.67
13. The Equitable Life Assurance Society of U.S. (N.Y.)	983	6,250 12,175	12.14 12.89
14. Mutual Benefit Life Insurance Co.	978	6,353 12,323	12.05 13.02
15. Republic National Life Insurance Co.	970	5,373 12,625	13.42 11.72
16. National Life Insurance Co. (Vt.)	963	6,314 12,854	13.17 12.19
17. The Canada Life Assurance Co.	898	5,425 11,675	13.06 12.60
18. Mutual Life Insurance Co. of New York [1]	1,029	6,500 12,500	12.91 13.22
19. State Mutual Life Assurance Co. of America (Mass.)	957	6,227 12,158	13.15 13.03

Company [7]	Annual Premium	Cash Value 10/20 Year	Cost Index 10/20 Year [6]
20. The Prudential Insurance Co. of America [1,2]	1,050	6,500 12,500	13.34 13.13
21. The Manufacturers Life Insurance Co.	846	5,200 11,475	13.50 13.06
22. The Lincoln National Life Insurance Co.	1,024	6,382 12,301	13.22 13.37
23. Crown Life Insurance Co. [2]	855	5,325 11,425	13.10 13.63
24. The Great-West Life Assurance Co.	904	5,600 12,000	13.31 13.53
25. The Guardian Life Insurance Co. of America	888	5,858 12,681	13.78 13.34
26. Continental Assurance Co. [3]	1,006	6,050 12,775	14.25 13.13
27. John Hancock Mutual Life Insurance Co. [3]	990	4,775 11,550	13.82 13.70
28. Occidental Life Insurance Co. of California	962	5,952 13,150	14.55 13.43
29. State Farm Life Insurance Co. [1,2]	1,008	5,738 12,066	14.38 13.77
30. Aetna Life Insurance Co.	1,043	6,250 12,375	15.70 12.91
31. Franklin Life Insurance Co.	990	5,691 12,136	15.22 14.64
32. American National Insurance Co. [1,2]	1,048	5,900 12,600	16.01 14.67
33. Metropolitan Life Insurance Co. [1,2]	1,053	6,225 12,700	16.23 14.73
34. Connecticut General Life Insurance Co.	980	6,400 12,650	14.38 16.83
35. The Western & Southern Life Insurance Co. [1,2,3]	1,026	4,575 11,475	14.63 17.51

MALE AGE 20 [4]—DATA FOR NONPARTICIPATING POLICIES
SOLD BY THE 20 LARGEST COMPANIES [5]
$10,000 STRAIGHT LIFE POLICY

Company [7]	Annual Premium	Cash Value 10/20 Year	Cost Index 10/20 Year [6]
1. The Travelers Insurance Co.[2]	$118	$ 910	$4.50
		2,480	3.77
2. Southwestern Life Insurance Co.[2]	117	850	4.88
		2,410	3.91
3. The National Life & Accident Insurance Co.[2]	116	850	4.84
		2,360	4.03
4. Allstate Life Insurance Co.	109	740	4.97
		2,060	4.25
5. Washington National Insurance Co.[2]	119	923	4.51
		2,198	4.80
6. Occidental Life Insurance Co. of California	113	770	5.16
		2,120	4.48
7. Franklin Life Insurance Co.	114	757	5.34
		2,171	4.39
8. Crown Life Insurance Co.[2]	106	660	5.28
		1,870	4.53
9. Connecticut General Life Insurance Co.[3]	111	600	5.53
		2,100	4.33
10. Continental Assurance Co.	118	770	5.59
		2,210	4.62
11. The Lincoln National Life Insurance Co.[3]	114	663	5.33
		2,018	4.88
12. Nationwide Life Insurance Co.[2]	114	704	5.73
		2,121	4.52
13. American National Insurance Co.[1, 2]	120	770	5.67
		2,200	4.74
14. The Manufacturers Life Insurance Co.	104	580	5.75
		1,730	4.81
15. Provident Life & Accident Insurance Co.	109	640	5.75
		1,880	4.81
16. The Great-West Life Assurance Co.	106	600	5.78
		1,770	4.88
17. United Benefit Life Insurance Co.[1, 2]	116	700	5.75
		1,950	5.06
18. Aetna Life Insurance Co.	120	760	5.96
		2,180	5.01
19. Business Men's Assurance Co. of America	118	740	5.89
		2,060	5.17
20. Republic National Life Insurance Co	116	680	6.13
		1,910	5.41

MALE AGE 20 [4]—DATA FOR NONPARTICIPATING POLICIES
SOLD BY THE 20 LARGEST COMPANIES [5]
$25,000 STRAIGHT LIFE POLICY

Company [7]	Annual Premium	Cash Value 10/20 Year	Cost Index 10/20 Year [6]
1. Provident Life & Accident	$276	$2,675	$2.46
Insurance Co.		6,450	2.70
2. Southwestern Life	264	2,250	3.34
Insurance Co.[2]		6,200	2.54
3. Allstate Life Insurance Co.	255	2,300	2.83
		5,300	3.35
4. Continental Assurance Co.	219	1,475	4.03
		4,400	3.08
5. The Lincoln National Life	222	1,474	4.16
Insurance Co.		4,385	3.22
6. American National	295	2,300	4.26
Insurance Co.[1, 2]		6,300	3.49
7. The National Life & Accident	279	2,125	4.36
Insurance Co.[2]		5,900	3.55
8. Crown Life Insurance Co.[2]	233	1,550	4.35
		4,450	3.57
9. Occidental Life Insurance Co.	246	1,675	4.45
of California		4,825	3.59
10. Aetna Life Insurance Co.	282	2,300	3.91
		5,450	4.24
11. United Benefit Life	246	1,500	4.76
Insurance Co.[1, 2]		4,400	3.89
12. Republic National Life	263	1,675	5.16
Insurance Co.		5,425	3.52
13. Washington National	244	1,517	4.87
Insurance Co.[2]		4,486	3.92
14. Franklin Life Insurance Co.	276	1,892	4.98
		5,428	4.03
15. Nationwide Life	269	1,760	5.13
Insurance Co.[2]		5,302	3.92
16. Business Men's Assurance Co.	243	1,450	5.06
of America		4,325	4.12
17. The Travelers Insurance Co.[2]	265	1,775	4.93
		4,900	4.25
18. Connecticut General Life	273	1,500	5.33
Insurance Co.[3]		5,250	4.13
19. The Manufacturers Life	246	1,450	5.21
Insurance Co.		4,325	4.27
20. The Great-West Life	251	1,500	5.24
Assurance Co.		4,425	4.33

MALE AGE 35 [4]—DATA FOR NONPARTICIPATING POLICIES
SOLD BY THE 20 LARGEST COMPANIES [5]
$10,000 STRAIGHT LIFE POLICY

Company [7]	Annual Premium	Cash Value 10/20 Year	Cost Index 10/20 Year [6]
1. The Travelers Insurance Co.[2]	$191	$1,530	$6.69
		3,730	6.84
2. Allstate Life Insurance Co.	176	1,350	6.79
		3,250	7.11
3. Crown Life Insurance Co.[2]	174	1,290	6.89
		3,110	7.13
4. The National Life & Accident Insurance Co.[2]	191	1,490	6.99
		3,630	7.15
5. Southwestern Life Insurance Co.[2]	189	1,450	7.14
		3,620	7.01
6. Connecticut General Life Insurance Co.[3]	179	1,130	7.34
		3,260	7.34
7. Washington National Insurance Co.[2]	193	1,548	6.77
		3,466	7.92
8. Continental Assurance Co.	185	1,390	7.41
		3,470	7.34
9. Franklin Life Insurance Co.	184	1,367	7.45
		3,413	7.38
10. The Manufacturers Life Insurance Co.	170	1,200	7.42
		2,960	7.47
11. Occidental Life Insurance Co. of California	184	1,400	7.24
		3,340	7.67
12. Nationwide Life Insurance Co.[2]	184	1,343	7.49
		3,338	7.42
13. The Lincoln National Life Insurance Co.[3]	182	1,205	7.08
		3,191	7.94
14. The Great-West Life Assurance Co.	174	1,230	7.55
		3,030	7.62
15. American National Insurance Co.[1, 2]	195	1,420	7.61
		3,470	7.72
16. Provident Life & Accident Insurance Co.	177	1,240	7.80
		3,080	7.79
17. United Benefit Life Insurance Co.[1, 2]	189	1,330	7.70
		3,180	8.03
18. Aetna Life Insurance Co.	191	1,370	8.14
		3,420	8.07
19. Business Men's Assurance Co. of America	188	1,350	8.04
		3,250	8.36
20. Republic National Life Insurance Co.	186	1,300	8.18
		3,140	8.45

MALE AGE 35 [4]—DATA FOR NONPARTICIPATING POLICIES
SOLD BY THE 20 LARGEST COMPANIES [5]
$25,000 STRAIGHT LIFE POLICY

Company [7]	Annual Premium	Cash Value 10/20 Year	Cost Index 10/20 Year [6]
1. Southwestern Life Insurance Co.[2]	$433	$3,850 9,325	$4.86 5.10
2. Allstate Life Insurance Co.	422	3,925 8,375	4.31 6.06
3. Provident Life & Accident Insurance Co.	446	4,100 9,325	4.73 5.82
4. Continental Assurance Co.	381	3,050 7,550	5.48 5.50
5. American National Insurance Co.[1,2]	466	3,875 9,500	5.71 5.81
6. Aetna Life Insurance Co.	438	3,900 8,550	5.05 6.50
7. The Lincoln National Life Insurance Co.	388	3,041 7,532	5.78 5.79
8. Crown Life Insurance Co.[2]	396	3,100 7,550	5.78 5.92
9. The Travelers Insurance Co.[2]	428	3,425 8,050	6.05 6.56
10. Republic National Life Insurance Co.	426	3,225 8,525	6.69 6.00
11. Occidental Life Insurance Co. of California	416	3,225 7,925	6.33 6.42
12. Washington National Insurance Co.[2]	415	3,119 7,692	6.50 6.51
13. Business Men's Assurance Co. of America	404	3,000 7,400	6.53 6.58
14. The National Life & Accident Insurance Co.[2]	465	3,725 9,075	6.51 6.67
15. United Benefit Life Insurance Co.[1,2]	425	3,050 7,525	6.69 6.70
16. Nationwide Life Insurance Co.[2]	445	3,358 8,344	6.89 6.82
17. The Manufacturers Life Insurance Co.	412	3,000 7,400	6.88 6.93
18. The Great-West Life Assurance Co.	422	3,075 7,575	7.01 7.08
19. Franklin Life Insurance Co.	451	3,417 8,533	7.09 7.02
20. Connecticut General Life Insurance Co.[3]	442	2,825 8,150	7.14 7.14

MALE AGE 50 [4]—DATA FOR NONPARTICIPATING POLICIES
SOLD BY THE 20 LARGEST COMPANIES [5]
$10,000 STRAIGHT LIFE POLICY

Company [7]	Annual Premium	Cash Value 10/20 Year	Cost Index 10/20 Year [6]
1. The Manufacturers Life Insurance Co.	$313	$2,010 4,360	$15.21 17.23
2. The Great-West Life Assurance Co.	318	2,080 4,470	15.13 17.36
3. The National Life & Accident Insurance Co.[2]	344	2,300 5,050	15.46 17.47
4. Southwestern Life Insurance Co.[2]	339	2,200 4,920	15.75 17.40
5. Washington National Insurance Co.[2]	346	2,397 4,905	14.96 18.21
6. Continental Assurance Co.	332	2,180 4,870	15.76 17.49
7. Crown Life Insurance Co.[2]	332	2,110 4,520	15.75 17.96
8. Franklin Life Insurance Co.	332	2,140 4,792	16.03 17.70
9. The Travelers Insurance Co.[2]	348	2,290 5,060	16.02 17.92
10. United Benefit Life Insurance Co.[1, 2]	346	2,130 4,540	15.82 18.12
11 Connecticut General Life Insurance Co.[3]	333	1,850 4,600	16.15 18.47
12. The Lincoln National Life Insurance Co.[3]	336	1,929 4,518	15.75 19.00
13. American National Insurance Co.[1, 2]	362	2,250 4,910	16.41 18.58
14. Provident Life & Accident Insurance Co.	329	2,040 4,460	16.53 18.47
15. Nationwide Life Insurance Co.[2]	344	2,161 4,695	16.53 18.57
16. Occidental Life Insurance Co. of California	343	2,250 4,720	16.29 19.07
17. Aetna Life Insurance Co.	341	2,140 4,800	16.97 18.61
18. Business Men's Assurance Co. of America	340	2,130 4,590	16.91 19.15
19. Republic National Life insurance Co.	338	2,100 4,500	16.94 19.23
20 Allstate Life Insurance Co	343	2,130 4,590	17.24 19.48

MALE AGE 50 [4]—DATA FOR NONPARTICIPATING POLICIES
SOLD BY THE 20 LARGEST COMPANIES [5]
$25,000 STRAIGHT LIFE POLICY

Company [7]	Annual Premium	Cash Value 10/20 Year	Cost Index 10/20 Year [6]
1. Southwestern Life Insurance Co.[2]	$794	$ 5,850 12,650	$12.56 14.86
2. Continental Assurance Co.	730	5,125 11,125	12.77 14.82
3. Crown Life Insurance Co.[2]	761	5,125 11,050	13.53 15.59
4. The Lincoln National Life Insurance Co.	754	5,102 11,105	13.83 15.83
5. Occidental Life Insurance Co. of California	775	5,375 11,475	13.79 16.19
6. Republic National Life Insurance Co.	776	5,175 11,975	14.46 15.57
7. Aetna Life Insurance Co.	810	5,975 12,000	13.24 16.88
8. American National Insurance Co.[1, 2]	866	5,900 12,975	14.08 16.12
9. Provident Life & Accident Insurance Co.	823	6,025 12,650	13.62 16.58
10. Business Men's Assurance Co. of America	762	5,025 10,925	14.36 16.35
11. United Benefit Life Insurance Co.[1, 2]	808	5,100 11,025	14.40 16.41
12. Washington National Insurance Co.[2]	791	5,247 11,365	14.39 16.42
13. The Travelers Insurance Co.[2]	814	5,625 11,550	14.07 17.04
14. The Manufacturers Life Insurance Co.	769	5,025 10,900	14.67 16.69
15. The Great-West Life Assurance Co.	781	5,200 11,175	14.59 16.82
16 The National Life & Accident Insurance Co.[2]	847	5,750 12,625	14.98 16.99
17 Allstate Life Insurance Co.	840	6,050 11,800	14.22 18.36
18. Franklin Life Insurance Co.	820	5,350 11,980	15.67 17.34
19. Nationwide Life Insurance Co.[2]	844	5,402 11,736	15.93 17.97
20 Connecticut General Life Insurance Co.[3]	828	4,625 11,500	15.95 18.27

APPENDIX E

Comparing Term Life Insurance Policies

Term life insurance lends itself to reasonable comparison, since it does not accumulate cash value and only remains in force for a specified period. In the following charts life insurance companies (rated by volume of business in Pennsylvania during 1972–1973) are listed in descending order of cost for a twenty-year period. The cost index figure listed in each chart represents the annual cost of insurance (per $1,000 of face value) when a 4 percent interest factor is applied to the yearly premium of each. It should be noted that if a cost index was drawn on some other period of insurance ownership (other than twenty years), the results might be different.

Where a company's annual premium figure includes a waiver-of-premium for disability, it is marked with a superior figure [1] and the cost index has been adjusted to take this extra provision into account.

TWENTY-YEAR COST INDEXES FOR PARTICIPATING $25,000
FIVE-YEAR RENEWABLE-CONVERTIBLE TERM POLICIES
FOR MALES AT AGE 25

Company	20-Year Cost Index	1st-Year Annual Premium	20th-Year Annual Premium
Home Life Insurance Co. (N.Y.)	$3.63	$107	$183
Mutual Benefit Life Insurance Co.	3.78	107	177
The Prudential Insurance Co. of America [1]	3.80	101	196
New York Life Insurance Co.	3.80	112	185
State Mutual Life Assurance Co. of America (Mass.)	3.90	104	169
Massachusetts Mutual Life Insurance Co.	3.91	104	172
New England Mutual Life Insurance Co.	3.94	110	170
Union Mutual Life Insurance Co. of New York	4.00	125	204
The Mutual Life Insurance Co. of New York	4.01	122	198
The Equitable Life Assurance Society of the U.S. (N.Y.)	4.08	106	179
State Farm Life Insurance Co.[1]	4.11	116	164
National Life Insurance (Vt.)	4.12	120	192
John Hancock Mutual Life Insurance Co.	4.13	128	184
The Penn Mutual Life Insurance Co.	4.21	108	178
Provident Mutual Life Insurance Co. of Philadelphia	4.26	104	174
Bankers Life Co. (Iowa)	4.27	128	193
The Guardian Life Insurance Co. of America	4.29	108	176
Phoenix Mutual Life Insurance Co.	4.35	97	164
Connecticut Mutual Life Insurance Co.	4.38	108	173
American United Life Insurance Co.	4.40	108	175
Metropolitan Life Insurance Co.[1]	4.41	128	223
Confederation Life Association	4.49	100	147
Pacific Mutual Life Insurance Co.	4.59	119	197
The Minnesota Mutual Life Insurance Co.[1]	4.69	113	186
Nationwide Life Insurance Co.	5.13	123	207

Company	20-Year Cost Index	1st-Year Annual Premium	20th-Year Annual Premium
The Canada Life Assurance Co.	4.22	93	138
Sun Life Assurance Co. of Canada	4.30	94	140
Crown Life Insurance Co.	4.54	102	143
Republic National Life Insurance Co.	4.67	104	153
Manufacturers Life Insurance Co.	4.69	104	152
United Benefit Life Insurance Co.[1]	4.70	110	160
Northwestern National Life Insurance Co.[1]	4.75	108	164
The Travelers Insurance Co.	4.79	107	165
American General Life Insurance Co.	4.83	110	159
Connecticut General Life Insurance Co.	4.86	108	163
Jefferson Standard Life Insurance Co. (N.C.)	4.89	106	165
Washington National Life Insurance Co.	4.91	106	165
The United States Life Insurance Co. in the City of N.Y.	4.93	100	172
Southwestern Life Insurance Co.	4.98	106	166
Great-West Life Assurance Co.	5.07	112	168
Life Insurance Co. of North America	5.08	112	166
Investors Syndicate Life and Annuity Co.	5.08	115	169
Continental Assurance Co.	5.26	115	169
American National Insurance Co.[1]	5.30	115	180
Life Insurance Co. of Virginia [1]	5.30	115	184
Fidelity Union Life Insurance Co. (Texas)	5.32	108	185
Business Men's Assurance Co. of America	5.35	115	177
Provident Life & Accident Insurance Co.	5.42	113	186
Aetna Life Insurance Co.	5.52	123	180
The National Life & Accident Insurance Co.	5.75	125	187

TWENTY-YEAR COST INDEXES FOR PARTICIPATING $25,000
FIVE-YEAR RENEWABLE-CONVERTIBLE TERM POLICIES
FOR MALES AT AGE 35

Company	20-Year Cost Index	1st-Year Annual Premium	20th-Year Annual Premium
Home Life Insurance Co. (N.Y.)	$6.30	$132	$357
Massachusetts Mutual Life Insurance Co.	6.44	132	337
Mutual Benefit Life Insurance Co.	6.49	136	346
State Farm Life Insurance Co.[1]	6.49	132	362
New York Life Insurance Co.	6.51	142	378
National Life Insurance Co. (Vt.)	6.65	147	386
State Mutual Life Assurance Co. of America (Mass.)	6.66	128	343
John Hancock Mutual Life Insurance Co.	6.67	167	352
The Prudential Insurance Co. of America	6.71	146	408
New England Mutual Life Insurance Co.	6.73	135	346
Bankers Life Co. (Iowa)	6.79	154	368
Phoenix Mutual Life Insurance Co.	6.82	116	343
Union Mutual Life Insurance Co.	6.89	159	388
Confederation Life Association	6.97	116	292
The Mutual Life Insurance Co. of New York	7.00	151	413
The Penn Mutual Life Insurance Co.	7.02	137	350
Provident Mutual Life Insurance Co. of Philadelphia	7.10	133	344
American United Life Insurance Co.	7.16	134	360
The Equitable Life Assurance Society of the U.S. (N.Y.)	7.16	136	356
The Guardian Life Insurance Co. of America	7.19	134	355
Connecticut Mutual Life Insurance Co.	7.26	132	347
The Minnesota Mutual Life Insurance Co.	7.61	142	375
Pacific Mutual Life Insurance Co.	7.66	151	388
Metropolitan Life Insurance Co.[1]	7.75	172	446
Nationwide Life Insurance Co.	7.93	160	392
The Canada Life Assurance Co.	6.67	112	297

Company	20-Year Cost Index	1st-Year Annual Premium	20th-Year Annual Premium
Crown Life Insurance Co.	6.72	115	268
Sun Life Assurance Co. of Canada	6.84	112	285
Manufacturers Life Insurance Co.	7.18	120	296
Republic National Life Insurance Co.	7.26	118	303
Northwestern National Life Insurance Co.[1]	7.49	128	349
United Benefit Life Insurance Co.	7.50	133	347
American General Insurance Co.	7.75	132	324
Connecticut General Life Insurance Co.	7.82	134	319
Jefferson Standard Life Insurance Co. (N.C.)	7.85	126	330
Southwestern Life Insurance Co.	7.91	130	332
Life Insurance Co. of North America	7.96	136	329
Continental Assurance Co.	7.96	137	321
Washington National Life Insurance Co.	7.99	126	340
Great-West Life Assurance Co.	7.99	130	334
The Travelers Insurance Co.	8.19	131	356
The United States Life Insurance Co. in the City of N.Y.	8.22	132	347
Investors Syndicate Life and Annuity Co.	8.25	136	346
Business Men's Assurance Co. of America	8.28	140	336
American National Insurance Co.[1]	8.33	141	372
Aetna Life Insurance Co.	8.48	141	350
Life Insurance Co. of Virginia [1]	8.50	145	370
The National Life & Accident Insurance Co.	8.75	150	352
Provident Life & Accident Insurance Co.	8.84	142	362
Fidelity Union Life Insurance Co. (Texas)	8.88	143	372

TWENTY-YEAR COST INDEXES FOR PARTICIPATING $25,000
FIVE-YEAR RENEWABLE-CONVERTIBLE TERM POLICIES
FOR MALES AT AGE 45

Company	20-Year Cost Index	1st-Year Annual Premium	20th-Year Annual Premium
The Prudential Insurance Co. of America [1]	$12.46	$275	$842
Massachusetts Mutual Life Insurance Co.	13.66	235	739
John Hancock Mutual Life Insurance Co.	13.82	292	776
Home Life Insurance Co.	13.91	247	779
National Life Insurance Co. (Vt.)	13.94	266	870
New York Life Insurance Co.	14.06	262	817
Phoenix Mutual Life Insurance Co.	14.06	262	817
State Mutual Life Assurance Co. of America (Mass.)	14.15	235	778
Mutual Benefit Life Insurance Co.	14.17	242	760
Bankers Life Co. (Iowa)	14.24	256	786
Confederation Life Association	14.36	203	662
New England Mutual Life Insurance Co.	14.45	242	797
The Mutual Life Insurance Co. of New York	14.72	276	889
The Penn Mutual Life Insurance Co.	14.77	244	772
State Farm Life Insurance Co.[1]	14.85	231	830
Union Mutual Life Insurance Co.	14.89	375	832
The Guardian Life Insurance Co. of America	14.95	244	762
Provident Mutual Life Insurance Co. of Philadelphia	15.05	238	751
Connecticut Mutual Life Insurance Co.	15.19	239	782
The Equitable Life Assurance Society of the U.S. (N.Y.)	15.53	247	793
The Minnesota Mutual Life Insurance Co.[1]	15.81	258	741
Nationwide Life Insurance Co.	16.16	279	832
Pacific Mutual Life Insurance Co.	16.26	270	852
Metropolitan Life Insurance Co.[1]	16.35	307	872
Crown Life Insurance Co.	13.37	192	616
The Canada Life Assurance Co.	13.87	197	640

Company	20-Year Cost Index	1st-Year Annual Premium	20th-Year Annual Premium
Sun Life Assurance Co. of Canada	14.07	201	647
Manufacturers Life Insurance Co.	14.63	206	666
Republic National Life Insurance Co.	14.78	210	664
Northwestern National Life Insurance Co.[1]	15.51	226	715
Continental Assurance Co.	15.71	227	704
United Benefit Life Insurance Co.[1]	15.73	242	717
American General Life Insurance Co.	16.18	231	738
Connecticut General Life Insurance Co.	16.20	232	768
Jefferson Standard Life Insurance Co. (N.C.)	16.27	228	742
Great-West Life Assurance Co.	16.38	232	740
Business Men's Assurance Co. of America	16.40	237	734
Southwestern Life Insurance Co.	16.46	226	754
American National Life Insurance Co.[1]	16.64	248	751
Life Insurance Co. of North America	16.65	238	780
Washington National Life Insurance Co.	16.79	235	790
Life Insurance Co. of Virginia [1]	16.84	258	748
Investor's Syndicate Life and Annuity Co.	16.84	252	751
The National Life & Accident Insurance Co.	17.16	250	764
The United States Life Insurance Co. of America	17.19	238	792
Aetna Life Insurance Co.	17.45	242	816
Provident Life & Accident Co.	17.46	264	765
Fidelity Union Life Insurance Co. (Texas)	17.47	261	725
The Travelers Insurance Co.	18.03	248	842

State Insurance Commissioners

Though the great bulk of the nation's life insurance business is transacted by companies with licenses to sell in every state, no federal agency has meaningful jurisdiction in policy enforcement and financial accountability matters (the Federal Trade Commission can intervene when false or misleading advertising claims are transmitted over state lines). Thus most insurance regulations are state regulations to be enforced by the equivalent of an insurance commissioner. Listed below are the addresses of the chief insurance regulators for all fifty states and the District of Columbia. While the capability and zeal of insurance commissioners varies greatly from state to state, all correspondence with insurance companies regarding problems or complaints should include a copy to the state office charged with regulating the industry.

Superintendent of Insurance
Alabama Insurance Department
Room 453
Administrative Building
Montgomery, Ala. 36104

Director of Insurance
Alaska Insurance Department
Room 410 Goldstein Building
Pouch "D"
Juneau, Alaska 99801

Director of Insurance
Arizona Department of Insurance
1601 West Jefferson
Phoenix, Ariz. 85007

Commissioner of Insurance
Arkansas Insurance Department
400 University Tower Building
Little Rock, Ark. 72204

Commissioner of Insurance
California Insurance Department
600 S. Commonwealth Ave.
Los Angeles, Cal. 90005

Commissioner of Insurance
Colorado Insurance Department
106 State Office Building
Denver, Colo. 80203

Commissioner of Insurance
Connecticut Insurance Department
State Office Building
165 Capitol Avenue
Hartford, Conn. 06115

Commissioner of Insurance
Delaware Insurance Department
Dover, Del. 19901

Superintendent of Insurance
District of Columbia
Insurance Department
614 H St., N.W.
Washington, D.C. 20001

Commissioner of Insurance
Florida Insurance Department
The Capitol
Tallahassee, Fla. 32304

Commissioner of Insurance
Georgia Insurance Department
State Capitol
Atlanta, Ga. 30334

Commissioner of Insurance
Hawaii Insurance Department
P. O. Box 3614
Honolulu, Hawaii 96911

Commissioner of Insurance
Idaho Insurance Department
206 State House
Boise, Idaho 83707

Director of Insurance
Illinois Insurance Department
525 West Jefferson St.
Springfield, Ill. 62707

Commissioner of Insurance
Indiana Insurance Department
509 State Office Building
Indianapolis, Ind. 46204

Commissioner of Insurance
Iowa Insurance Department
Lucas State Office Building
Des Moines, Iowa 50319

Commissioner of Insurance
Kansas Insurance Department
State Office Building
Topeka, Kan. 66612

Commissioner of Insurance
Kentucky Insurance Department
Old Capitol Annex
Frankfort, Ky. 40601

Commissioner of Insurance
Louisiana Insurance Department
Box 44214, Capitol Station
Baton Rouge, La. 70804

Superintendent of Insurance
Maine Insurance Bureau
State House Annex
Capitol Shopping Center
Augusta, Me. 04330

Commissioner of Insurance
Maryland Insurance Division
1 South Calvert St.
Baltimore, Md. 21202

Commissioner of Insurance
Massachusetts Division of Insurance
100 Cambridge St.
Boston, Mass. 02202

Commissioner of Insurance
Michigan Insurance Bureau
111 North Hosmer St.
Lansing, Mich. 48913

Commissioner of Insurance
Minnesota Insurance Department
210 State Office Building
St. Paul, Minn. 55101

Commissioner of Insurance
Mississippi Insurance Department
910 Woolfolk Building
P. O. Box 79
Jackson, Miss. 39205

Superintendent of Insurance
Missouri Division of Insurance
Department of Business and Administration
P. O. Box 690
Jefferson City, Mo. 65101

Commissioner of Insurance
Montana Insurance Department
Capitol Building
Helena, Mont. 59601

Director of Insurance
Nebraska Insurance Department
1335 L St.
Lincoln, Neb. 68509

Commissioner of Insurance
Nevada Insurance Division
Department of Commerce
Nye Building
Carson City, Nev. 89701

Commissioner of Insurance
New Hampshire Insurance Department
78 N. Main St.
Concord, N.H. 03301

Commissioner of Insurance
Department of Banking and Insurance
201 E. State St.
Trenton, N.J. 08625

Superintendent of Insurance
New Mexico Insurance Department
P. O. Drawer 1269
Santa Fe, N.M. 87501

Superintendent of Insurance
New York Insurance Department
123 William St.
New York, N.Y. 10038

Commissioner of Insurance
North Carolina Insurance Department
P. O. Box 26387
Raleigh, N.C. 27611

Commissioner of Insurance
North Dakota Insurance Department
State Capitol
Bismarck, N.D. 58501

Director of Insurance
Ohio Insurance Department
447 E. Broad St.
Columbus, Ohio 43215

Commissioner of Insurance
Oklahoma Insurance Department
Room 408
Will Rogers Memorial Office Building
Oklahoma City, Okla. 73105

Commissioner of Insurance
Insurance Department
Department of Commerce
158 12th St., N.E.
Salem, Ore. 97310

Commissioner of Insurance
Pennsylvania Insurance Department
108 Finance Building
State Capitol
Harrisburg, Pa. 17120

Commissioner of Insurance
Rhode Island Insurance Division
169 Weybosset St.
Providence, R.I. 02903

Commissioner of Insurance
South Carolina Insurance Department
Federal Land Bank Building
1401 Hampton St.
Columbia, S.C. 29201

Commissioner of Insurance
South Dakota Department of Insurance
Capitol Building
Pierre, S.D. 57501

Commissioner of Insurance
Tennessee Department of Insurance
114 State Office Building
Nashville, Tenn. 37219

Commissioner of Insurance
Texas Insurance Department
1110 San Jacinto St.
Austin, Tex. 78701

Commissioner of Insurance
Utah Insurance Department
115 State Capitol
Salt Lake City, Utah 84114

Commissioner of Insurance
Vermont Insurance and Banking Department
State Office Building
Montpelier, Vt. 05602

Commissioner of Insurance
Virginia Insurance Department
700 Blanton Building
P. O. Box 1157
Richmond, Va. 23209

Commissioner of Insurance
Washington Insurance Department
Insurance Building
Olympia, Wash. 98501

Commissioner of Insurance
West Virginia Insurance Department
1800 E. Washington St.
Charleston, W.Va. 25305

Commissioner of Insurance
Wisconsin Insurance Department
212 N. Bassett St.
Madison, Wisc. 53703

Commissioner of Insurance
Department of Insurance
State of Wyoming
500 Randall Ave.
Cheyenne, Wyo. 82002

Glossary

ACCIDENTAL DEATH BENEFITS—A provision which may be added to a life insurance policy so that if death results from an accident the policy pays an additional benefit above the face amount of the policy. When the additional benefit equals twice the face amount of the policy, it is often referred to as "double indemnity."

AGENT—A representative of an insurance company with authority to sell the policies of that company. Insurance agents are often referred to as underwriters.

AME—In Social Security, average monthly (taxable) earnings up to the point of death, disability, or retirement of a covered worker, used to help compute the actual benefit received.

ANNUITY—A contract usually sold by life insurance companies in which a sum of money is guaranteed to be paid at regular intervals for a certain period of time in exchange for a lump-sum payment of money. Usually the payments of an annuity last for the life of a specific person. If the payments are to continue for a certain number of years without regard to a particular person's death, they are called an annuity certain.

AUTOMATIC PREMIUM LOAN—The automatic payment of the premium of a life insurance policy from a loan from the cash value of the policy if the premium has not been paid by the end of the grace period.

BENEFICIARY—The person who is named in an insurance policy to receive the proceeds of the policy in the event the insured dies.

BENEFITS—The amount of money an insurance company promises to pay under a particular insurance policy.

BROKER—A sales representative who usually sells insurance of various kinds for more than one company.

CANCELLATION—The terminating of an existing policy before it would normally expire.

CASH SURRENDER VALUE—The value of an insurance policy if the insured terminates the policy or surrenders it to the insurance company.

CASH VALUE LIFE INSURANCE—A phrase used to describe life insurance in which the premium remains level for the entire pay period and which accumulates a value as the policy becomes older.

CLAIM—A demand to an insurance company that an insurance payment is due as stipulated in a policy.

COINSURANCE—A policy provision which specifies that the insurance company and the policyholder will share in the expenses of a particular loss.

CONVERTIBLE TERM INSURANCE—Term insurance that can be exchanged for a cash value policy without evidence of insurability.

CREDIT LIFE INSURANCE—Life insurance issued by a lender to cover payment of a loan or installment purchase if the policyholder should die.

DEDUCTIBLE—The amount of money you must pay before your insurance benefits begin. The insurer will only pay benefits on losses above the amount of your deductible.

DISABILITY INSURANCE—A type of health insurance paying certain expenses resulting from disablement, bodily injury, accidental death, and sickness.

DIVIDEND—A return of money to the policyholder of participating insurance policies for overcharges of premiums.

DIVIDEND ADDITION—Paid-up insurance which is added to the face amount of a policy and which is paid for by a dividend from the policy.

DOUBLE INDEMNITY—See ACCIDENTAL DEATH BENE-FITS.

ENDORSEMENT—An addition to a policy designating a change from a normal reading of the contract.

ENDOWMENT INSURANCE—Cash value insurance which is designed to mature during the life of the insured. If the insured dies before the endowment policy matures, the beneficiary receives the face amount of the policy. If the insured lives until the policy matures, he receives the face amount of the policy at that time.

EXCLUSIONS—Items in policies designating specific illnesses, hazards, or circumstances for which you are not covered.

EXTENDED TERM INSURANCE—A nonforfeiture option available when a cash value policy is surrendered. It provides for term insurance equal to the face amount of the surrendered policy for a period of time dependent upon the cash surrender value of the policy being surrendered.

FACE AMOUNT—The amount of money that will be paid to a beneficiary in the event of the insured's death or which will be paid to the insured if he is alive at the time the policy matures.

FIDUCIARY—One who holds something in trust for the benefit of another. Every pension plan must execute written documents providing for one or more "named Fiduciaries" who have the authority and responsibility for managing the operation of the plan.

FUNDING—The adding of money or assets to a pension account to insure the ability to pay benefits. All federally insured pension plans must receive funding contributions from the employer based upon a minimum schedule provided by the government.

GRACE PERIOD—A period of time (usually 30 or 31 days) after the date a premium on an insurance policy is due during which the policy remains in force and the premium still may be paid without penalty.

GROUP INSURANCE—Insurance, usually issued through employers and unions, which covers a group of persons.

GUARANTEED RENEWABLE CLAUSE—An insurance policy provision guaranteeing that the policy will be kept in force if you continue to pay your premiums on time.

INCONTESTABLE CLAUSE—A policy clause that provides that after a specified period (usually two years) after a policy has been in force the insurer has no right to dispute any statements made in the original application.

INDEMNITY POLICY—A health insurance policy which pays the insured a specified amount each day or week. Generally, benefits are paid only for hospitalization and not for medical or outpatient care.

INDUSTRIAL LIFE INSURANCE—Life insurance in which the face amount of the policy is usually less than $1,000 and on which the premiums are collected weekly or monthly at the home of the insured by an agent of the insurance company.

INSURANCE—Protection against the financial hazards of specific events.

INSURANCE COMPANY—Any corporation which sells insurance protection to the public.

IRA—"Individual Retirement Account"—an account, usually with a bank as trustee, into which a worker who does not participate in a qualified pension plan may contribute as much as $1,500 per year—tax-free—for accumulation and investment purposes. Funds contributed and their earnings may be drawn upon retirement at 59½ years of age, or disability at any age.

JUDGMENT—A court decision that determines the rights and obligations of parties to a lawsuit.

LAPSED POLICY—An insurance policy which has been terminated by the insurance company because the premiums have not been paid.

LIFE EXPECTANCY—The average number of years a person at a certain age is expected to continue living.

LIMITED PAYMENT LIFE INSURANCE—Whole life insurance in which the premiums are paid only for a certain number of years.

MUTUAL FUND—A corporation without a fixed capitalization, selling and buying its own shares. A mutual fund uses its capital to invest in the securities of other companies.

PARTICIPATION—The right, in pension plans, to begin accumulating pension benefits as an employee. Various pension plans differ as to necessary qualifications to become eligible, including age and required waiting period.

PBGC—Pension Benefit Guaranty Corporation, an agency of the U.S. government which insures to pension plan participants the payment of their benefits if the qualified plan is terminated.

POLICY—A written document which contains the terms of an insurance contract.

POLICY LIMIT—The maximum amount of money an insurance company will pay under a particular policy.

POLICY LOAN—A loan made by an insurance company to the owner of a cash value insurance policy in which the cash value of the policy is pledged as security.

PORTABILITY—The possibility of transferring one's accrued pension benefits from one pension plan to another. This can take many forms, including that of company plan to IRA, company plan to another company plan, IRA to company plan, etc.

PREMIUM—The payment that is made for an insurance policy.

RATED POLICY—An insurance policy on which the premiums are higher than usual owing to the insurance company's determination that the insured represents a higher risk than other persons his age.

RENEWABLE TERM INSURANCE—Term insurance which can be renewed without evidence or insurability for a certain number of successive terms or until the insured reaches a certain age.

RESERVE—A sum of money that an insurance company sets aside to insure that it can make payments on future claims.

REVIVAL—Reinstatement of a lapsed insurance policy.

SCHEDULE—A list of specific maximum amounts payable for certain conditions.

SETTLEMENT OPTIONS—Options contained in an insurance policy which provide methods by which the proceeds of the policy may be paid.

STOCK INSURANCE COMPANIES—Insurance companies which are owned by shareholders and organized to make profit.

STRAIGHT LIFE INSURANCE—Cash value life insurance on which the premiums are paid for the life of the insured.

TERM INSURANCE—Insurance which insures the life of the insured for a specific period of time.

VARIABLE LIFE INSURANCE—Life insurance in which a stated amount of money is payable at the death of the insured but which may pay more money depending upon how investments made with a portion of the premiums fare.

VESTING—The scheduling under which an employee participating in a pension plan becomes entitled to benefits he cannot lose. Becoming fully "vested" in a pension plan, then, is to acquire pension rights which can be taken by an employee even if he should leave a company before retirement. Under the 1974 Pension Reform Act, an employee benefit must be fully vested after fifteen years of service. This rule becomes effective in January 1976.

WAITING PERIOD—The specified number of days after the policy is issued during which the policyholder is not covered.

WAIVER OF PREMIUM—An option in a life insurance policy which provides that the premiums on the policy do not have to be paid if the insured becomes permanently and totally disabled.

WHOLE LIFE INSURANCE—Insurance which covers a person for his entire life and which pays the beneficiary no matter when the insured dies.

Index

Index